P9-BJX-176

emotions
A Brief History

"In this short history, Keith Oatley captures the current excitement of the ongoing 'Affect Revolution' and its historical antecedents. As psychologists seek to decipher the foundations of the many emotional values of animate existence, they should not forget the many historical roots from which the current blossoming of research is emerging. This gem helps put the field in perspective." *Jaak Panksepp, Bowling Green State University* and author of *Affective Neuroscience*

"There are dozens of books on emotions these days, but none like Oatley's new work. This original, wide-ranging, erudite, yet accessible romp through the centuries of thought and feeling about emotion as encountered in literature, philosophy, religion, politics, history and anthropology, is a tour de force. A consummate work by one of the leaders in the field of emotions research, it is not only a scholarly work of tremendous breadth, but a literary achievement in its own right – Oatley is a master of the well-turned phrase and the work is rich in wry musings and penetrating insight." *Carol Magai, Long Island University, Brooklyn Campus*

"Oatley's beautifully written book comes out of his deep knowledge both of the history of thought and of the most up-to-date research in the science of emotions ... a masterly introduction to philosophical and scientific thinking about the emotions in personal and social life. It's all done with Oatley's characteristic lucidity, his light touch, and his novelist's gift for vivid illustration.... this book will afford fresh insights and original perspectives to delight even seasoned scholars." *Ronnie de Sousa, University of Toronto*

Blackwell Brief Histories of Psychology

The *Blackwell Brief Histories of Psychology* offer concise, accessible, and lively accounts of key topics within psychology, such as emotion, intelligence, and stress, that have had a profound effect on psychological and cultural life. The books in this series provide a rich sense of historical context while remaining grounded in contemporary issues and research that will be of interest to both academic and general readers.

Stress: A Brief History
Cary L. Cooper and Philip Dewe

Evolutionary Thought in Psychology: A Brief History
Henry Plotkin

Emotions: A Brief History
Keith Oatley

Intelligence: A Brief History
Anna T. Cianciolo and Robert J. Sternberg

emotions

A Brief History

KEITH OATLEY

© 2004 by Keith Oatley

BLACKWELL PUBLISHING
350 Main Street, Malden, MA 02148-5020, USA
108 Cowley Road, Oxford OX4 1JF, UK
550 Swanston Street, Carlton, Victoria 3053, Australia

The right of Keith Oatley to be identified as the Author of this
Work has been asserted in accordance with the UK Copyright,
Designs, and Patents Act 1988.

All rights reserved. No part of this publication may be reproduced,
stored in a retrieval system, or transmitted, in any form or by any
means, electronic, mechanical, photocopying, recording or
otherwise, except as permitted by the UK Copyright, Designs, and
Patents Act 1988, without the prior permission of the publisher.

First published 2004 by Blackwell Publishing Ltd

Library of Congress Cataloging-in-Publication Data

Oatley, Keith.
Emotions: a brief history / Keith Oatley.
p. cm.— (Blackwell brief histories of psychology)
Includes bibliographical references and index.
ISBN 1-4051-1314-6 (hardcover : alk. paper)—
ISBN 1-4051-1315-4 (pbk : alk. paper)
1. Emotions—History. I. Title. II. Series.

BF531.017 2004
152.4'09—dc22
2004005400

A catalogue record for this title is available from the British Library.

Set in 10/12pt Book Antique
by Kolam Information Services Pvt. Ltd, Pondicherry, India
Printed and bound in the United Kingdom
by TJ International Ltd, Padstow, Cornwall

The publisher's policy is to use permanent paper from mills that operate
a sustainable forestry policy, and which has been manufactured from
pulp processed using acid-free and elementary chlorine-free practices.
Furthermore, the publisher ensures that the text paper and cover board
used have met acceptable environmental accreditation standards.

For further information on
Blackwell Publishing, visit our website:
http://www.blackwellpublishing.com

To Kathleen, Jennifer, and Hannah

Contents

List of Illustrations

Preface

The heart has its reasons of which
reason knows nothing
Blaise Pascal, *Pensées*

What might we want from a history of emotions? By exploring
our past, we can reach a deeper understanding of our emotions
in the present. For emotions, history has three meanings. The first
is evolutionary. Aspects of our emotions derive from millions of
years ago when our pre-human ancestors became more successful than members of other pre-human species who did not
survive because those others were less well equipped in their
emotional and practical repertoires than were our ancestors. The
repertoire that was successful in the past has been passed by
human genes on to us in the present. The second meaning is
the personal history of each of us: how our emotions develop
from birth, through the relationships of childhood and across the
life span. The third sense is the ordinary one: a history of ideas
and social movements. How in our culture have emotions been
understood? How did they affect people then, and how do they
affect us now?

In this book, I explore with the reader some of the ways in
which the threads of these three senses of history intertwine.
Darwin proposed that emotional expressions derive from the
evolutionary past of our species. So, for instance, in evolutionary
terms, each of us inherits from forebears a tendency to bond with
another person over a long period in a more-or-less exclusive
sexual union. The adaptive purpose of the arrangement, so
paleontologists tell us, was to ensure the male would help to
bring up offspring who were likely to be genetically his own. In
terms of individual history, our ability to love is affected by the
history of our experience of being loved during our own infancy.
In terms of the history of culture, a long-lasting sexual union is

reflected in many societies in the idea of marriage. Ideas of emotions now in the West are quite different from what they were just a few hundred years ago. Then a wife was typically a kind of property of a male head of a household. Now in Western societies, spouses expect to be affectionate companions.[1]

Somewhat overstepping the usual boundaries of history, I also take us into the research of the first years of the twenty-first century. The topics of the new research continue the threads of history. They include therapy of emotions, questions of reconciliation, neuroimaging of the brain during emotional states, social effects of emotions, biographies based on emotional themes, gene–environment interactions, and emotional intelligence.

Although in some ways we humans distrust emotions, we also believe they embody our most important values. If you want to know what people value, listen to their stories. In particular, listen to the underlying emotional themes. To do this in the West, you need merely turn on the television. You need not flick through many channels before you reach a story of two people in love or of some sad person who has lost someone loved. Flick a bit further and you come (in fiction or in the news) to a story of someone who has been wronged and who pursues a perpetrator to exact an angry vengeance. Love and anger, indeed, are core themes of many, perhaps most, stories in the West.[2] We visit and revisit them perhaps because these issues resonate with our deeper valuing of human lives in the face of vicissitudes that hinder our longings. We revisit them also perhaps because we can't quite understand the problematic nature of these emotions. These engaging resonances and these problems point to love and anger being issues that are close to the core of ourselves. If it is emotions – rather than predominantly rationality or technology or economic relations – that make for the humanness of our human world, how do they affect our understanding of ourselves and others?

Acknowledgements

I am grateful to Brian Stock for his introductions to the history of emotions in a course we taught together on the topic at the University of Toronto. I especially thank Jennifer Jenkins, who gave helpful editorial suggestions throughout, as she does with all my books, and also Gerald Cupchik and Sholom Glouberman, who read a draft of the manuscript and gave useful comments. I also thank for their helpful comments on drafts of specific chapters: Jaak Panksepp (Chapter 4), Carol Magai (Chapter 6), and Peter Salovey (Chapter 8). I thank Phyllis Wentworth, Philip Carpenter, Christine Cardone, and Sarah Coleman of Blackwell Publishing for their encouragement and help, Justin Dyer for his copy editing, as well as two anonymous readers of a draft of this book for their suggestions.

CHAPTER ONE

Meaning and Ambiguity

Emotions: Signals of What is Vital

Elizabeth Barrett Browning, photo about 1850, after her marriage to Robert Browning. Source: *US Library of Congress.*

Persisting Preoccupations

Here, from some 150 years ago, are the first lines of a famous poem.

> How do I love thee? Let me count the ways.
> I love thee to the depth and breadth and height
> My soul can reach...[1]

Elizabeth Barrett wrote the famous opening lines of this sonnet when she was 39. She had been an invalid for the previous seven years, the result of a broken blood vessel. Robert Browning wrote to her in January 1845, in admiration of her highly regarded *Poems* published a year earlier. In May he came to visit, and met her.

Elizabeth lived in London, in the house of her father, who had forbidden her to marry. For more than a year Elizabeth and Robert exchanged clandestine letters. At first she refused his proposals of marriage, thinking he would not need an invalid wife. But her health steadily improved, and the couple did marry – secretly – in St Marylebone Church in September 1846. A week later, Elizabeth left her father's house, never to return. The Brownings went to live in Italy, where they had 15 happy years together. Elizabeth's father never forgave her. He returned all her entreating letters unopened.

Towards the end of her sonnet, which probably was composed in 1846, Elizabeth writes: "I love thee with a passion put to use / In my old griefs..." These griefs included the death of a much loved brother, Edward, who drowned while sailing.

Love is an emotion with an individual history of coming to know another person. Of all the events that ordinarily happen to ordinary people, in the West at least, falling in love has the most momentous effects. It is a hinge on which an individual history can turn. It is often the occasion for finally leaving the parental home, for making a commitment for life to another person, for taking on new responsibilities, enclosing that person within the circle of self so that his or her welfare becomes as important as one's own. Elizabeth Barrett's poem and her own love story have helped us to understand it better.

Love is an emotion that has a history in the evolution of human beings, in each individual, and in the development of Western culture. It is an emotion that helps to define who we human beings are. "Some people," said La Rochefoucauld, "would never have fallen in love if they had never heard of love."[2] This may be an understatement. Without stories of falling in love and of being in love in the modern Western sense, we might not know how to conduct this important emotion.

What is an Emotion?

Love is an example of an emotion, but what is an emotion?[3] This question was asked by William James, father of American psychology, in 1884.[4] The answer around which this book is based was proposed nearly two and a half millennia ago in Greece, and is today widely accepted. It is that emotions are most typically caused by evaluations – psychologists also call them appraisals[5] – of events in relation to what is important to us: our goals, our concerns, our aspirations.

Emotions may include bodily changes such as a glow and smile of happiness, the pounding heart of anxiety, the clenched fist of anger. Indeed, William James argued that an emotion *is* the perception of any such bodily change.[6] The common idea that when we see a bear in the woods, we are frightened and therefore run is quite wrong, said James. We see the bear and run. The fear is the perception of our body arousing itself for the emergency and moving to escape. Although the evidence to support the order of events that James postulated is somewhat equivocal, most modern theorists accept that emotions involve both mind and body.

The term "emotion" covers a wide range of phenomena. To denote this range some writers have revived the terms "affect" and "affective," which had been used in English in the early seventeenth century.[7] More commonly nowadays, however, the terms "emotion" and "emotional" are used to denote this range.

The kind of emotion that is most commonly experienced occurs somewhat suddenly. We feel suddenly happy when, at the airport, we greet a friend whom we've not seen for some time. Or we may feel anger at a slight. Such an emotion fills our consciousness. It might best be called a reactive emotion, though it's often just called an emotion.

Emotions are based on what we know, and they include thoughts, sometimes obsessive thoughts, about what has happened or what might happen next. Emotions also often create in us urges to act in an emotional way in relation to someone else: we might feel an urge to hug that person or to stomp out of the room. Emotions give life its urgency. They are, as Nico Frijda has said, states of immediate readiness to act.[8] Though the smile when we first see our friend, or a frown of anger, lasts only a few seconds, the thoughts of an emotion, the tone of feeling happy, angry, or whatever it may be, and the urge to act, may last for minutes or hours.

The family of emotional phenomena includes yet longer lasting processes that may best be called moods, such as cheerfulness, irritability, or sadness, which may persist for hours or days. Unlike reactive emotions, which usually have causes that are obvious to us, moods can be of uncertain provenance.

What one may call sentiments – the term was once more common than now – last even longer. Love of the kind Elizabeth Barrett wrote about, or distrust of a kind that we may feel towards someone whom we experience as acting only for his or her own ends, are sentiments: long-lasting emotional states of relating to other people. They can form the central bases of a relationship over many years.

Preference is another term in the emotion family: one may think of it as a silent emotion waiting for an opportunity to express itself in a choice we make.

Are there different kinds of emotion? I believe there are. We experience both anger and sadness as negative, but they are distinct.[9] Friendly affection is distinct, too. It is perhaps our most human emotion: the most recently evolved, perhaps the most fragile. It contributes to the scripts of love, cooperation, and kindness. Without it, the human world as we know it would not exist.

The Workings of Emotions

Let us move now from what emotions are to how they work, keeping in mind both reactive emotions and longer lasting sentiments. Reactive emotions occur when the appearance of the world as we assume it to be[10] is pierced by reality. In our assumed world, objects and people take on the colors of our understandings, of our hopes, of our desires, of our likes and dislikes. A reactive emotion occurs with the unexpected; it is a meeting of what we assumed with what we did not assume.

Whilst living a life of solitude, we meet someone who stirs us. Or, without in any way expecting it, an acquaintance surprises us with an act of great generosity. The world suddenly intrudes through the layers of our assumptions.

Of what is our assumed world composed? The shape is of what is there: the trees, our friends, our colleagues at work. But each of the objects and people we see is also made from how we construct it. As Hippolite Taine said:

> So our ordinary perception is an inward dream which happens to correspond to things outside; and, instead of saying that a hallucination is a perception that is false, we must say that perception is a *hallucination that is of the truth*.[11]

We know from dreams that our brains have the machinery to make scenes that we experience. So eyes are not windows that let in aspects of the world. Instead they pick up clues to enable us to construct the world as we experience it. The clues are used, along with our assumed and implicit knowledge of the way the world works, to construct what we perceive.

Reactive emotions are caused when something in the assumed world unexpectedly affects a concern. Sometimes the unexpected is delightful, and we have the sense of new possibilities. Sometimes the unexpected is painful: in anger, for instance, the world narrows to plans of how we might confront the offender with the offense.

We can think of reactive emotions and sentiments respectively as like the two kinds of neural signal by which our muscles work: phasic signals move a limb; the signals of muscle tone hold the limb steadily in place. Comparably, a reactive emotion causes a change whereas a sentiment maintains an emotional attitude. Think of both, in the way suggested by Michel Aubé, as commitments.[12] In the understanding of emotions, the idea of commitment is as important as the ideas of evaluation and readiness. Commitments are the bases of our relationships. So a reactive emotion is typically a change of commitment, and a sentiment is a maintained commitment. Falling in love is a change, a commitment to a new person. Love is a maintained commitment to a person. Anger is typically a reaction to something that has happened, and a commitment to resolving, in one way or another, the conflict that it promotes.

Emotions of both shorter and longer durations are signals to ourselves and others. Emotions are signals to ourselves that steer us towards those things we evaluate as worthwhile in our projects, away from what would be deleterious. They are signals to others, because although these others have no direct access to our inner feelings, they notice our reactive emotions and sentiments. And – constituted like us – they can infer what we may be feeling. So: as evaluations, emotions are guides, to us and to others. As commitments, they are the sinews and articulations of our relationships.

Emotions and the History of Writing

There is something problematic about our emotions. Is that why they have been at the center of stories all round the world? When we pick up a book of non-fiction we hope to be informed, but when we pick up a book of fiction, or hear a poem, or go to a play or film, we expect to be moved.

It was in the civilization of Sumer, in present-day Iraq, that writing was first invented. We in the West and the Middle East, are the direct descendants of this culture. Some 5,000 years ago the ephemeral shadows of thought first took lasting shape in writing. From this culture what do we read? We read stories of emotions. In one text written about 3,800 years ago, the goddess Inanna wants Gilgamesh in sexual union: "O lord Gilgamesh, you shall be my man, I will not let you go . . ." Gilgamesh rejects her, so the goddess asks her father if she may take the Bull of Heaven, with which she will avenge herself on Gilgamesh.[13]

Not long after the epic tales of Gilgamesh, stories began to be written in Africa. From the writings of the Middle Kingdom of Egypt, for instance, comes a sad story called "The dispute between a man and his *Ba* [soul]," in which the man says he is weary of life. Made angry by his complaints, his soul threatens to leave him.[14] Then the man delivers four poems, the lines of which include:

> To whom shall I speak today?
> No-one is cheerful,
> He with whom one walked is no more.

To whom shall I speak today?
I am burdened with grief
For lack of an intimate

To whom shall I speak today?
Wrong roams the earth,
And ends not.

The man's soul says he should throw his complaints on the woodpile, but agrees to stay with him.

A thousand years later, the stories of the Hebrews were written. They recount that, when God created the world and human beings, almost the first thing that happened was an emotion. Eve, and then Adam, ate of the fruit of the tree of knowledge of good and evil. At the moment of becoming conscious, knowing good and evil, they became self-conscious, and they felt ashamed.[15]

Written at around the same time, the first substantial surviving fiction of the Greeks was *The Iliad,* which starts with these words: *Menin aeide, thea* – "Of rage sing, goddess." The poet invokes the muse to sing of the rage of Achilles against Agamemnon, the commander in chief of the Greek army. This very personal emotion, of the Greeks' best warrior, aroused because of a slight, nearly destroyed the Greek army.

There are writings of similar antiquity from the Asian continent. These include the *Mahabharata,* a story of family feuding that allegorizes the battle of good and evil. The heroes represent the good. They triumph, and rejoice. But they suffer a final remorse because they too have committed evil in their fight.[16]

In China, which has a similarly ancient written tradition, the sage Confucius wrote about emotion as long ago as the fifth century BC. Around 200 years later, his follower, Mencius, continued the theme, for example in the story of a king who asked him about the qualities needed in a ruler. The king had seen a bull shrinking in fear when about to be sacrificed. He told his attendants to spare the bull, and use a lamb instead. Mencius says that he is sure that the king had been moved by compassion at seeing the bull's distress, and that quality would be sufficient to make him a good king. The king said: "For though the deed was mine, when I looked into myself I failed to understand my own heart. You described it for me and your words struck a chord in me."[17]

In the Americas, the European Conquistadors overthrew the civilizations of the Aztecs, the Incas, and the Maya in the first part of the sixteenth century. Of the indigenous groups, the Maya seem to have possessed the most literate culture, but only four pre-conquest Mayan books in their original hieroglyphic script have survived. To the intense distress of the Maya, the books were burned by the Spanish on the grounds that "they contained nothing but superstition and the devil's falsehoods."[18]

A few writings did survive by being transcribed into alphabetic script after the conquest, perhaps most famously the *Popol Vuh*, a Mayan Genesis.[19] It tells of the gods' four experiments to make humans. On the first try, the beings had no arms, so could not work. On the second, a being was made out of mud, but not only could it not keep its shape but, being solitary, it could not reproduce. The third try was to make people out of wood. Though the resulting beings looked and talked like humans, they could not remember "The heart of the Sky" (the gods), so the gods destroyed them by means of a flood. Their remnants are the monkeys. In their fourth experiment, to make humans out of food, the gods were at last successful. Four human ancestors, androgenous "mother-fathers," were made. They did pray to their makers, but they exceeded the gods' expectations: "Perfectly they saw, perfectly they knew everything under the sky, whenever they looked."[20] The gods thought this was not good, because, as they put it: "their deeds would become equal to ours."[21] Therefore the new humans were

> ...blinded as the face of a mirror is breathed upon. Their eyes were weakened. Now it was only when they looked nearby that things were clear. And such was the loss of the means of understanding, along with the means of knowing everything.[22]

Descendants of ancient European civilization might be reminded of the plays of Aeschylus and Sophocles – some centuries after Homer – in which humans could act but could not foresee some of the most important results of their actions. Or was the clouding of human vision a blinding by emotions?

Stories based on emotions as human universals

How, with such contrasts between love and cruelty, can the history of human emotions be anything other than problematic? The story of Elizabeth Barrett and Robert Browning is a love story in the classical sense. Love stories are the most common kinds of stories worldwide, and stories of warring contention are the second most common.[23] In the canonical love story, two strangers meet. More or less quickly they fall in love, and they long to be together, but their union is prevented. In Elizabeth Barrett's case her father forbade the marriage.

In the happy version of such stories, the couple contend with the obstacles, and overcome them; Elizabeth's and Robert's story is of this kind, though a sad chord is heard of Elizabeth's continuing estrangement from her father. In the tragic version of such stories, some event such as death separates the lovers. In *Romeo and Juliet,* one of the most famous love stories in the West, the death of both lovers is transcended symbolically by a union between the two families whose feud had militated against the lovers' marriage.

Love itself has changed in the course of historical time. If you were to hear now of a father forbidding his 39-year-old daughter to marry, you would be shocked. You would regard the father's possessive emotions as inappropriate. He should feel – we would say – quite differently. In other words, our idea of love and even its experience in relation to parents and to partners has changed. So emotions are not fixed. They are made in part from what we know culturally, and from what we believe to be socially appropriate.

The classic story of love that meets vicissitudes continues, though with transformations. In the circle of my acquaintances in the past two years, I know of one couple in which the woman was Muslim and the man Christian. The fathers of both these people had a difficult tussle with themselves accepting their daughter's and son's union, but at the wedding each father read a piece of scripture from his tradition. Another person I know, a woman very close to her parents, told them she loved another woman. The parents could not bring themselves to speak to her for two months, and remained upset about their daughter's preference.

Why have emotions been so fascinating to writers?

Why should emotions have been so fascinating in the 5,000-year history of writing? It is because they are about our concerns. Though we tend to forget brief emotions within a few minutes, our larger emotions are markers of our most important concerns and aspirations, and we do remember them. In this way, love is momentous. It signifies the accomplishment of a longing, the possible union with just that other with whom one can become intimate. In a survey of 100,000 Americans, psychologist Jonathan Freedman found that it was not wealth, or health, or worldly success, that most people regarded as the most important ingredient of happiness. It was love in marriage.[24]

So emotions are fascinating because the more substantial of them point to what is most important to us as human beings. Reactive emotions occur when a concern, a project, an aspiration, has fared either better or worse than we had expected. Elizabeth Barrett had resigned herself to life as a recluse. Instead she was surprised to find someone who loved her and whom she could love to the depth and breadth and height her soul could reach. Positive emotions – love, happiness, pride in accomplishment, relief – occur as signals that things are going well, or better than expected. Negative emotions – anger, fear, sadness, shame, contempt – occur when we evaluate things as going worse than we expect, when our goals and projects fail, or are frustrated, when someone behaves worse than we anticipate.

A second reason why emotions are fascinating is that they set us puzzles. Love may be wonderful to lovers, but its paradoxes include the way in which it can nullify all previous commitments. Its effects may be less than wonderful to other people. Of all the objects in our mental life, emotions are among the most mysterious. Many human emotions seem paradoxical. Their implications may reach beyond what we can easily think through.

Here is an instance from a young British woman aged 20, whom I shall call Abigail.[25] She kept an emotion diary at my request, looking out for, and making notes on, emotions as they occurred in her everyday life. When she gave me back the diary, I interviewed her to ask more about the incidents. One emotion was anger in an argument with her boyfriend. There seemed nothing mysterious. She rated her anger's intensity as 7 on a scale of 0 ("not noticeable") to 10 ("the most intense I have experienced in my life"). The argument had started about preferences for different kinds of music. Initially it had lasted about two-and-a-half hours. Then its perplexing aspects began. For three nights she had recurrences of anger, which kept her awake. She said: "I just couldn't get through to him." It made her ask herself, "Is this going too far?" and "If this goes too far, it [the relationship] would end." A serious conclusion seemed to be implied by what had started as a simple matter. She said that her behavior included sarcasm, cutting remarks, and sulking. But she also made attempts at reparation. She had emotions about her emotion. She felt guilty, she said, and wondered if she was pressing her boyfriend too hard. Not only should one not have such feelings, but she was, she said, "a person who would not be irritated by someone with a different opinion." And, she said, her anger included "something that lowered [her] estimation of [herself] on some kind of internal scale." The emotion too seemed to have a history: the argument "reminded her of an ex-boyfriend" and made her "wonder if it [the relationship] was worth it." This in turn made her not like her current boyfriend, and think that he had faults. She thought she should step back and think about the incident some more, as a way of calming down. Then she thought she was partly to blame.

Abigail's anger was a signal to herself to think about her identity. It hinted at a trait that she may have had but did not like, which perhaps had caused problems earlier in her history, which had previously made it difficult to keep close to a previous boyfriend, and which was now raising a comparable problem again.

Abigail's feelings and thoughts were particular to her, but are not such sequences recognizable? When an emotion breaks through the layers of our expectations, upheavals of thought[26] may occur, and we may find ourselves searching for reasons and implications of what happened. Emotions can drive thoughts and ruminations in an involuntary way. They can keep us awake at night. They can distract us from other things that we are doing. They can return unwilled. In the more important matters of life, the upheaval of an emotion can become an earthquake.

The Inchoateness of Some Emotions

Although we know exactly what most reactive emotions are about, some emotions may start as vague and formless.[27] In a short story first published in *Vogue* magazine in 1894, the American writer Kate Chopin depicted an emotion of a woman, Louise Mallard, that started indistinctly. The story starts with her hearing that her husband has died in a train crash.[28] Unlike some people, who are simply benumbed by such news, she wept at once, in her sister's arms. The event was distinct, and her bereavement caused the emotion. But when the first storm of grief had subsided, Louise Mallard went to her room. She found herself looking from her window at the sky, and then she began to experience another emotion.

> There was something coming to her and she was waiting for it, fearfully. What was it? She did not know; it was too subtle and elusive to name. But she felt it, creeping out of the sky, reaching towards her, through the sounds, the scents, the color that filled the air. Now her bosom rose and fell tumultuously. She was beginning to recognize this thing that was approaching to possess her . . . [29]

The emotion, when it became conscious, was a joy at the realization of her freedom. She may have loved her husband, but he also constrained her.

Emotions can point to goals and concerns. Sometimes they are clear to us. Sometimes, however, we might not know we have these goals, so the emotions associated with them emerge only slowly. Sometimes, as with Louise Mallard, concerns are hidden from us because they would be difficult to own. When such a meaning emerges from some unknown region, it tells us something. It can cause further emotions, which can open new worlds or make us question firmly held convictions.

Emotions point to matters of vital importance, and energize us in relation to them. What is most important in human life? For the most part and for most people, the answer is: other people. So emotions include love, anger, affection, shame, fear, contempt. They set our priorities, make our lives meaningful, and create our commitments to friends or against enemies. When a reactive emotion or a mood points to concerns or aspirations that we barely recognize in ourselves, it may set us problems. The urgency it confers on these problems may act as a goad.

An emotion can be a tug on the sleeve. Sometimes it can be a violent shove, or a painful kick. It demands to be noticed, it demands to be understood. Emotions' properties as indicators of importance and as setters of problems make them the most fascinating aspects of mental life, both our own and that of those about whom we care.

Emotions and Creativity: The Era of Romanticism

If emotions can be setters of problems, in their very nature they can challenge our creativity. They fairly demand that we think anew on the unexpected event that caused them, and on its implications. Their insistence ensures that we concentrate. Not only that: many people do indeed find creative solutions to the problems that their emotions set them.[30]

The idea of emotions as our most authentic spurs to creativity is the core of an influential theory of art, one of the best accounts of which was given by Robin Collingwood, in 1938. He said that art was not entertainment, or the craft of working with particular materials to achieve certain effects. Art is – quite simply – the expression of emotions. He did not mean expression as one might frown in anger, or smile in happiness. He did not mean simply giving a label to an emotion, for instance, "I'm rather envious of her." What he meant was exploring an emotion in its particularity, and in detail. Imagine a man, says Collingwood:

> At first he is conscious of having an emotion, but not conscious of what this emotion is. All he is conscious of is a perturbation or excitement, which he feels going on within him, but of whose nature he is ignorant. While in this state, all he can say about his emotion is: "I feel... I don't know how I feel." From this helpless and oppressed condition he extricates himself by doing something which we call expressing himself. This is an activity which has something to do with the thing we call language: he expresses himself by speaking. It also has something to with consciousness: the emotion expressed is the emotion of whose nature the person who feels it is no longer unconscious.[31]

The man of whom Collingwood speaks is the artist: not necessarily in the professional sense, but the artist in all of us. Expression of an emotion in this sense occurs as a person explores its meaning and implications. Expression occurs in a language, often of words, but it might be in painting, or in music. Emotions and sentiments are often latent. The meanings of Abigail's emotion emerged in the days after she had been angry at her boyfriend. In her short story, Kate Chopin depicted an emotion emerging gradually as from a mist. Often, it is by expressing them in words (including the words of conversation), images, symbols, or music that emotions take shape, so that their significance becomes clearer.

Romanticism

The theory that Collingwood expounded was the Romantic theory of art.[32] The beginning of the era of Romanticism is generally dated to 1750, when Jean-Jacques Rousseau wrote a prize-winning essay on whether the restoration of the arts and sciences at that time had contributed to the purification of morals.[33] His conclusion was no. The arts, and especially the art of manners, were artificial. He wrote that they tended therefore to obscure natural feelings, and recognition of the feelings of others; this artificial turn led to a deterioration of morals.

Romanticism was the mood of both the American and French Revolutions at the end of eighteenth century. The argument – no, the feeling – at the beginning of the Romantic period was that people are naturally sociable. Therefore society does not need, in the American case, the imposition of a colonial power thousands of miles away, or, in the French case, a monarchy to impose servitude on a populace. Rousseau wrote: "Man is born free, but is everywhere in chains."

In literature there was a corresponding move away from the contrived and the artificial, towards the natural and towards a primacy of emotions, so that William Wordsworth, writing in 1802, was able to define poetry as:

> The spontaneous overflow of powerful feelings: it takes its origin
> from emotion recollected in tranquillity: the emotion is contem-
> plated till by a species of reaction the tranquillity disappears,
> and an emotion, kindred to that which was before the subject of

contemplation, is gradually produced and does itself actually exist in the mind.[34]

In English, there are many great novels of the early Romantic period, and they reflect a high valuation of emotions. One might read Jane Austen's *Pride and prejudice*. The title points to the importance of the emotions. The book is about Elizabeth Bennet, who at first is repelled by the arrogant manners of a certain Mr Darcy who enters her neighborhood. She gradually learns more about him, and recognizes her own prideful prejudice in her judgments both of him and of another man who had given an initially more favorable impression. The novel is a kind of anti-Hollywood love story. In Hollywood, we know how love is portrayed. Two people, typically strangers, see each other. Their eyes meet. They stare at each other for several long seconds. Snap: they are in love. Jane Austen, whose teenage writings included fierce satire on what she regarded as the silly love stories of her time, proposed a different idea: Elizabeth can only love Darcy by getting to know him, and who he is in the layers beneath his manners.

Since the beginning of Romantic period, emotions have been seen as bases for poetry, novels, music, and visual arts, which can therefore be thought of as repositories of reflections on these aspects of life that give it meaning but also cause so many of our problems.

In terms of our relations with the emotions, we are still very much in the Romantic era. The questions raised by Jane Austen's novels, for instance of the conflicts between artificiality and naturalness, and between love at first sight and knowing someone as they are, could scarcely be more contemporary. If you doubt whether we are still in the era of Romanticism, what do you make of the modern belief that life should be lived with intensity, with heart, and with style? All three are watchwords of Romanticism.

Have Emotions Changed in the Course of Historical Time?

Many historians date the beginning of the modern world to the beginning of the Renaissance, around 1300, with Dante in Florence and his masterpiece *The divine comedy*. Have emotions changed between medieval times and modern? And have there been changes in the tenor of emotional life, even of the experience of emotions, during the 700 years of modernity? These questions have not been among the most researched within the academic discipline of history, but they have been investigated. One widely accepted idea is that in medieval times people were more expressive of emotions than now. A famous statement of the idea began Johan Huizinga's *The waning of the Middle Ages*:

> To the world [at the end of the medieval period], the outlines of all things seemed more clearly marked than to us. The contrast between suffering and joy, between adversity and happiness, appeared more striking. All experience had yet to the minds of men the directness and absoluteness of the pleasure and pain of child-life.[35]

Another famous work was Norbert Elias's *The civilizing process*,[36] in which he saw powerful people in medieval times as violent and wild because they had nothing to restrain them. Then domestication began. From the twelfth century onwards, the courts of great aristocrats imposed constraints by means of the presence of noble ladies. Knights began to devote themselves, in love that was often – or at least sometimes – chaste, to ladies of high station.[37] "Courtesy, courtship, courtliness," are terms that derive from ideas of how to behave at court. What happened according to Elias, was that emotions that were not wild, notably shame, and institutions of wider reach than the court, notably the modern state, began to impose restraint. Continuing in the tradition of investigating changes of emotions over time, the historians Peter and Carol Stearns introduced the term "emotionology," and have explored in many publications the idea of how in America since the nineteenth century various unpleasant emotions have been controlled. Peter Stearns has argued that today the USA's biggest ambivalence is between increasing indulgence in hedonistic pleasures, on the one hand, and increasing efforts of repression of emotions, on the other.[38]

Behind such ideas as those of Huizinga, Elias, and the Stearnses is a widely held piece of folk theory. Folk theory is the implicit theory we all use to explain to ourselves and to others how the world works. The piece of folk theory at issue sees emotion as something like a liquid heated in a pot that is liable to boil over. For Huizinga and Elias, medieval emotions boiled over freely and frequently. For Peter Stearns, modern America is caught between taking the lid off and clamping it down. The idea is that with historical time, the issue of how emotions can be contained, or, to use a modern term, regulated, has come to concern both society and individuals.

William Reddy has explored how emotions are both the target and the expression of large changes in society.[39] He introduces the idea of what he calls emotives: forms of speech and action that bring into being what they refer to. Thus anger, or saying, "I'm completely fed up with you," is an emotive that brings into being a state of reciprocal anger in the person who is addressed. Reddy's main object of study is the French Revolution, in which the idea of generosity of all to all was proposed to replace the repressive monarchist society, and did indeed, for a short time, come into being. Reddy argues that by means of its emotives every society sets up an emotional regime, within which certain expressions, for instance respect for authority, love of God, universal benevolence, or whatever it may be, are induced and maintained.

Reddy's idea is not that law makers prescribe certain behavior which is then carried out. Rather, within a particular emotional regime, laws are made to codify the emotives of the regime. Strict regimes such as occur in totalitarian states enforce their standards rigidly, and some people's personal styles benefit from having their emotional lives tightly managed. Other more relaxed regimes enforce strictness only in sections of society such as the army. In America today, we might notice how emotives have been used to induce hostility to "terrorism." A collective fear and a collective anger have occurred, with all that these mentalities involve.[40]

Other historians also started to examine changes in more intimate aspects of life. Lawrence Stone examined the huge changes that have took place in the family in the early modern period in England.[41] In 1500, for both rich and poor, death was omnipresent. Neither children nor parents were expected to live long. There was less parental investment in children. The idea of childrearing was often to break the will of a child, as a horse is broken in order to be ridden. Adult populations were produced that were both more subservient to authority and also more paranoid than today. At the same time sexual relationships were vastly delayed as compared with those elsewhere in the world, and perhaps this resulted in the diversion of energy into work. The replacement of patriarchal marriage by companionate marriage, the appearance of privacy, the discovery of sexual pleasure by the married couple: all these began to come into their own in Europe and America only towards the end of the eighteenth century and the beginning of the nineteenth. At the same time, the new nuclear family enabled the devotion of parents to bringing up children in affection. At the beginning of the twenty-first century we have moved not necessarily in universal practice, but in principle, to families in which coercion is pathology,[42] in which all family members expect openness, trust, communication, and a degree of equality. Anthony Giddens has said:

> When we apply these principles [such as equality, openness, trust] – as ideals, I would stress again – to relationships we are talking of something very important – the possible emergence of what I shall call a democracy of the emotions in everyday life. A democracy of the emotions, it seems to me, is as important as public democracy in improving the quality of our lives.[43]

Among some historians such as Reddy and Stone a trend is noticeable: away from ideas of emotions as inhering largely in individuals (another piece of folk theory, to which the idea of boiling liquid is related) towards ideas that the principal effects of emotions are social.

Emotions are the underlying structures both of our more public and of our more intimate relationships. The creativity to which we are invited by emotions depends on the society in which we live, and the ideas and concepts of such societies change with time. During a lifetime each of us may begin to make sense of the patterns of our emotions. We can come to think not so much of what to do about our own individual experience, as of how to understand and take part in the emotions of the communities to which we belong.

CHAPTER TWO

Evolution, Culture, and a Necessary Ambivalence

Inherited Repertoires of Emotion Built Upon by Culture and Experience

Young woman smiling: a photo from Darwin's 1872 book on emotions, which was one of the first works to use photography for a scientific purpose. Source: *C. Darwin (1872).* The expression of the emotions in man and animals. *London: Murray, Plate III.*

Darwin and His Influence

Charles Darwin published his great book on evolution, *On the origin of species by means of natural selection*, in 1859. Not long after it came out, the wife of the Bishop of Worcester is said to have remarked: "My dear, descended from the apes! Let us hope it is not true, but if it is let us pray it does not become generally known."[1]

The Bishop's wife had not got it quite right. We are not descended from the creatures we think of as apes – chimpanzees, bonobos, gorillas, and orang-utans – but we do share common ancestors with them. The human line diverged from the line that led to modern chimpanzees and bonobos about six million years ago. But the Bishop's wife was almost right, and her fears were confirmed. Our evolution from ape-like ancestors is true. It has become one of the most generally known pieces of science.

In 1836, Darwin had returned from a voyage of nearly five years during which he was the naturalist on HMS *Beagle*. Two years after his return, he married his cousin, Emma Wedgwood. He inherited enough money so that he did not need a paying job. He was something of a workaholic, and he published many books. He was socially shy, and almost his only excursions from home were to spas in attempts to cure his mysterious illnesses. The long and happy marriage between Charles and Emma saw the births of ten children, and many evenings of high spirits playing backgammon together.

Darwin and evolution

The idea of biology with which Darwin started, with which almost anyone would start in Victorian times, was that God had created separately each species of plant and each species of animal. Species were unchanging. God had, moreover, created human beings not only as a separate species, but in his own image. On his return from his voyage, Darwin started a series of notebooks. His notes included observations that features of the physical world had changed since the earth's formation, for instance because of corals and volcanoes. So if certain animals and plants were fitted to the new environments caused by these changes, Darwin started to think that they too must have changed. And since, on a remote set of islands, there were several species of finches not seen anywhere else in the world, then these species may have come into being when a small population of the birds became isolated and then changed to fit different environmental niches on the islands. Darwin thought more and more deeply on such matters until he reached the conclusions that became his theory of evolution. It is a theory with profound implications for how we understand emotions.

Darwin concluded that three principles drive evolution. One principle he called superabundance: in every species many more offspring are produced than survive to adulthood. The second was variation: each offspring is somewhat different from all others, in ways that can be passed on by heredity to its own offspring. The third was selection: those offspring whose variations fitted them more closely to their current environment tended to survive and reproduce, and hence to transmit to the next generation those traits that had so fitted them. Over immense periods of time, and working according to these principles, as changes became more extreme, certain populations of plants and animals could become so different from those from which they had developed that they became new species. That's it: Darwin's theory of evolution. On reading the theory, Thomas Huxley, who would become Darwin's chief expositor, said: "How extremely stupid not to have thought of that." More recently, one eminent scholar has said it's the best idea anyone ever had.[2]

Darwin and emotions

Darwin's idea of evolution itself took some years to evolve. It did not stand alone. It was deeply embedded in his ideas about the human relation to other animals and the relation of minds to brains. One idea that engaged him was that as well as sharing anatomical and physiological features with other mammals – a backbone, four limbs, live births of immature infants who are suckled with their mother's milk – we share with them traits of behavior and mentality. In particular, human emotions are not only similar in humans all round the world, but some of them are similar to those of other animals. Like domestic cats and dogs, we can get frightened. Like them, we can become angry. Like them, we want to be close to other members of our species.

We humans like to believe that we make decisions, and act according to our thoughts, our understanding, our logic. What, then, do we make of this experiment that Darwin carried out on himself at the London Zoo?

> I put my face close to the thick glass-plate in front of a puff adder in the Zoological Gardens, with the firm determination of not starting back if the snake struck at me; but, as soon as the blow was struck, my resolution went for nothing, and I jumped a yard or two backwards with astonishing rapidity. My will and reason were powerless against the imagination of a danger which had never been experienced.[3]

Human reason failed. Darwin knew with certainty that the snake could not reach him through the thick plate glass. In leaping "a yard or two backwards," his will and reason "went for nothing." Something else caused his behavior: an "imagination of a danger which [he] had never ... experienced."

Darwin suggested that what controlled his behavior had been installed in the brain long ago: a brain process to make him leap backwards when a snake struck. By degrees our animal ancestors had acquired (by Darwin's principle of inherited variation), and themselves passed on, traits such as this one. In the distant past, many potential ancestors were born (Darwin's idea of super-abundance). Those who did not carry traits of jumping rapidly back from a striking snake were more likely to be killed by such snakes. They did not survive to reproduce (the effect of natural selection) and so were not our ancestors. The snake-escape reaction therefore come to be – in modern terms – programmed by our ancestors' genes into our nervous systems. It is there in all of us. Darwin had never previously experienced being struck at by a puff adder, but the program worked and he jumped back.

In 1872, Darwin published *The expression of the emotions in man and animals*, a book that he worked up from notes and observations he had been making for more than 30 years.[4] The principal conclusion of this book was that expressions of emotion in modern adult human beings (of which his leaping backwards was an example) can occur whether or not they are any use. Programs of emotional expression have been installed into our nervous systems in the course of evolution and they can operate even when, according to reason, there would be no need for them. One question raised by Darwin, then, is how much of our behavior derives not from "will and reason," as we might prefer to believe, but from properties of our nervous systems, including those of the emotions?

In the previous chapter, I described how the era of Romanticism began in the second half of the eighteenth century, in politics and in the arts. In the history of philosophical thinking about emotions in the West, there had been important books on emotions. Plato, Aristotle, Baruch Spinoza, and René Descartes all wrote influentially on the subject. But it was Darwin's books *On the origin of species* and *The expression of the emotions*, published more than a hundred years after the Romantic period had begun, that started an equivalent period in science, and psychologists began to consider how emotions are important in human lives.

The most direct successors of Darwin in the field of emotions have been a group of psychologists who have gathered evidence to indicate that certain expressions, such as smiling, frowning, and sneering, are, as Darwin supposed, human universals. The argument is that each is derived from a basic emotion with an evolutionarily adapted function. This work constitutes a vigorous tradition.[5] It runs alongside the tradition of cognitive science applied to emotions which stretches back to Aristotle's analyses of emotions as evaluations, which was applied to modern research by Magda Arnold.[6] There is a certain amount of tension between these two traditions, with the more biological group worrying about "cognitive imperialism" and proposing that emotion research should be thought of within its own field: "affective science."

Evolutionary history of emotions

In his book on emotions, Darwin used the term "expression" to mean any behavior or visible bodily change caused by an emotion. So his fearful backwards jump when the snake struck, or a smile of happiness, or a tear of sadness in the eye, were all expressions of specific emotions. Darwin's argument was that pieces of behavior had some of the features of pieces of our anatomy that had persisted even after they had become redundant. The appendix, in our digestive system, for instance, seems no longer to have a use. It is a vestige. Its main interest to us now is as a piece of evidence that we are evolved from former crea-tures in whom it did have a use. In the same way, Darwin pointed out that our body hair standing on end when we are frightened or angry nowadays has no use whatever. Animals from whom we are descended, much hairier than we are, would have their hair stand on end when angry or frightened. Thereby they would look bigger and more formidable. Evidently this expression was effective, for it is widespread among mammals. For us not-quite-hairless humans, the expression of our remaining body hairs standing on end no longer has a deterrent effect.

Nowadays, such evidence as the existence of the appendix, and of hair standing on end, is no longer critical to establishing that evolution occurred. Other aspects have become more im-portant. Comparably in understanding emotions, Darwin's thinking that emotions provide evidence for evolution has become less important than the question of how his theory of evolution helps us to understand ourselves as we are today. Evolution is a process of design. By generating variations, and preserving those that work, evolution mindlessly searches over the space of possibilities for how life might adapt to certain environments, including new ones. This process of design-by-nature is not good at making deletions. That is why we still have the appendix and still have our hair standing on end when we are angry or frightened. But it also creates and carries forward designs that have worked in the past and, perhaps with modifications, can work in the present. If we are to understand our emotions, we need to understand them as founded in earlier forms of life, even when these forms of life, and the environments to which they are adapted, no longer exist.

Individual emotional development

Just as Darwin argued that some adult emotions derive from earlier states in evolution, he argued that others derive from earlier states in the development of each individual child. For instance, he thought crying in adulthood derived from screaming and crying in infancy. Physical caresses are yet more interesting. They are valued enormously for themselves in the present day. But there is little doubt that they also derive from earlier expressions. This is what Darwin says:

A strong desire to touch the beloved person is commonly felt; and love is expressed by this means more plainly than by any other. Hence we long to clasp in our arms those whom we tenderly love. We probably owe this desire to inherited habit, in association with the nursing and tending of our children, and with the mutual caresses of lovers.[7]

The phrase "inherited habit" in this quotation means "genetically programmed action." But in the final parts of the sentence Darwin seems to get his own theory wrong. He should immediately have followed the phrase "inherited habit" with some clause such as, "in association with the way that, during infancy, we hug our mothers." Perhaps he was not quite able to write that adult caresses, including those of sexual love, may derive in part from childhood cuddling of a mother. This was certainly a Darwinian idea. Perhaps in a pre-Freudian age, consciously or unconsciously, Darwin was unable to commit it to writing.

The experience of an emotion transports us back into the unwritten history of the human race. Imagine a film star such as Denzel Washington or Julia Roberts. What makes the movie image attractive is a certain facial and bodily patterning that many thousands of years ago our genes specified as sexually inviting. Certainly the patterning has only a little to do with the actual Denzel or the actual Julia. What you see is a two-dimensional image: few readers of this book are likely to meet these actual people. Nothing but a pattern of light on a screen induces our brain to generate the experience of being drawn towards them. The outline of such patterning was laid down in our evolutionary history. It works, as Darwin pointed out, whether or not it is any use.

Morality and Ambivalence

It is often said that one cannot derive an "ought" from an "is." If we accept Darwin's theory, this adage is false. We human beings value love, and we value its caresses. We think of love as among the highest expressions of being human. Yet like other emotions it is based in our evolutionary and personal history. If, instead of infantile cuddling of a mother, and if instead of clasping a lover in our arms in the act of procreation, we were members of a species of fish whose sperm were ejaculated into the water near where ovulation occurred, and whose offspring were never recognized by the parent, there would be no valuation of love and no thought of caresses.

Emotions are not just quirks and vestiges. They are as widespread among mammals as the possession of warm blood, four limbs, and the breathing of air. We must conclude that they have current and important uses, and that mammalian life is built around them. When we talk about the love of any mammalian mother for her offspring, or of an offspring's love for its mother, we talk about psychological facts as foundational as the physiological fact that mothers give breast milk to their infants.

Here is the problem. Just as we have inherited from hominid ancestors the ability to walk on two legs, so we inherited a repertoire of emotions. Nothing in modern life seems as valuable as some of these emotions. The sexualized love that enables partners to support each other affectionately over most of a lifetime, the parental love that enables children to be raised and protected, and the affectionate love of friends are celebrated as the very essence of humanity. At the same time, other emotions in our repertoire, such as the contempt we can feel for members of out-groups, may not just be handicaps: they can take murderous forms that may yet lead to the extinction of our species in the new environments we have created of cities, aircraft, the internet, and explosive weaponry.

In the first chapter, I described emotions as partly obvious, but partly ambiguous. In addition we recognize that emotions are sometimes useful but sometimes destructive. Appropriately, therefore, we are ambivalent towards them. Their ambiguity and our ambivalence make for a strong mix. Emotions are among our most important assets, but in some ways they contend against who we wish to be. From the ancient Greeks, from the temple at Delphi, comes the injunction: "Know thyself." Though the oracle did not make this entirely clear, what we should come to know are our emotional selves, our inner core.

Emotions and the environment of evolutionary adaptedness

Emotions came into being as solutions to certain kinds of problems in what Leda Cosmides and John Tooby call the environment of evolutionary adaptedness.[8] By this phrase, they mean a former way of life: the typical environment of our hominid ancestors for all but the last 10,000 of the last six million years.[9] Although we humans have concerns about physical events like forest fires and snowstorms, the world to which we are adapted was largely a social world of groups of a couple of dozen people, many of them genetically related. In the environment of human adaptedness such groups gathered food, ate together, and camped together. From time to time they would meet other groups who lived in the same region.

Richard Wrangham recounts how the fossil record shows that a huge change occurred in the line that led to humans about 1.9 million years ago with the emergence of a species called *Homo erectus*. Males of *Homo habilis*, their immediate forerunners, were more than 50 percent larger than females. By contrast, the males of *Homo erectus* were, like modern humans, only about 15 percent larger than females. They had smaller arms, longer legs, smaller teeth, and smaller guts. Their brains had not yet reached modern human size but were about 1,000 cc, almost double the size of *habilis* brains. Wrangham says that: "For the first time [in evolution] they could be put in clothes and given hats, and they could walk down a New York street without generating too many stares."[10]

Like many modern hunter-gatherers, our hominid ancestors would have obtained most of their nutrition from vegetable foods such as roots.[11] Our chimpanzee cousins also obtain most of their food from vegetable sources (fruits), but they also hunt small animals, principally colobus monkeys. So they include a proportion of meat in their diet. It seems likely that our ancestors also hunted small animals. Stone tools have been found from about 2.5 million years ago, and marks of such tools on the bones of larger animals, such as antelope, indicate that the people of that time were butchering them. In addition, the most striking aspect of Wrangham's hypothesis, but one that makes sense of many other aspects of the fossil record, is that about the time of the emergence of *Homo erectus*, there also emerged the means to control fire, and to cook, thus making root vegetables and meat more digestible.

People in all human societies cook food and share it. To do so enhances the warmth of companionship. It is tempting to think, too, that the human enjoyment of staring into the fire (often much to be preferred to the television) is an echo from nearly two million years ago. Fire has benefits in addition to its use for cooking: it is useful for scaring away large predators.

The argument of Cosmides and Tooby is that, as the title of an article they wrote in 1990 put it, "The past explains the present."[12] Emotions manage actions by detecting certain events related to goals that were important and that recurred frequently during evolution: successes, the thwarting of goals by others, threats, losses, and so forth. Each emotion, then, came to select a subset of the repertoire more or less appropriate to each of these principal kinds of event as it occurred.

Consider threats. When a threat occurs, a suite from our repertoire is selected. In fear, the mind becomes, as it were, specialized to deal with just this kind of event.[13] Here is part of the fear suite, brought into readiness when a threat is detected or expected. Stop what you're doing. Freeze. Check what you've just done. Concentrate on the threat, exclude all other issues. Scan the environment for potential information about the threat. Make expressions of social deference. Signal the presence of danger by making alarm calls to others. Prepare to escape. Prepare to fight. Not all these may occur in any one episode, but mind and body are prepared without deliberation by bringing into readiness this suite of potential actions. Consciously the mental tone of this preparedness is fear, or the sustained mood of anxiety.

Nico Frijda has defined types of emotions as different types of action readiness, each of which gives priority to one set of concerns rather than to others.[14] So, emotions select suites of actions: make them ready and indeed urgent, in reaction to distinctive kinds of circumstance. These suites have been bundled together as selected by evolution, and these bundles derive from what we experience as distinct emotions. Populations without such suites have not survived. If we take the adage of Tooby and Cosmides – "the past explains the present" – and run it backwards, we can look at what we recognize as modern emotions – happiness, love, sadness, anger, and so on – and project them back into the past. What must the human environment of evolutionary adaptedness have been like to make these emotions useful?

We can infer that the most important aspect of that environment would have been the world of companions. It must have been one in which people were made happy by being with friends, close relatives, lovers. Just as now, our ancestors were concerned for their children, concerned that friends and loved ones liked them, upset if something, or someone, they valued was lost or taken. The species from which we are descended had members who made close relationships with each other that allowed them to commit themselves to plans, and to become sad when the plans did not work out. Our ancestors faced threats from the natural world, including those from large carnivores, as well as from certain other members of the social group: either kind could invoke the suite of fearful preparations and actions. We can infer that our ancestors easily took offense, and became angry if their position in the social structure was not recognized. And though affectionate to members of the in-group, our fore-bears had a tendency to treat members of out-groups, perhaps other hominid species or members of our own species who were estranged or different, with contempt and sometimes with murderous aggression.

Most modern humans live in fixed habitations. Relatively few members of our species now move nomadically between sea-sonal camping sites. We tend to live closely with a small number of intimates in our household (sexual partner and children) rather than in extended families, as did our forebears. In the last few hundred years we have invented privacy. But our emotions still guide us in relation to our immediate social world.

Two cultures' attitudes to anger and aggression

In her book *Never in anger*, Jean Briggs gives a fascinating anthro-pological account of the emotional tenor of a way of life that may approximate some of our ancestors. It describes her stay between June 1963 and March 1965 with a family of the Utku: a society of Inuit who lived on the banks of Back River as it enters Chantry Inlet, on the edge of the Arctic Circle, about 1,300 miles north of Winnipeg, Canada. The head of the family was Inuttiaq, who adopted Briggs. His wife was Allaq. They lived with three chil-dren, and a fourth was born during her visit. During the long cold winter, she shared the family *iglu*. During the summer the family camped with several other families at a fishing spot beside the river.

In the Utku group among whom she lived, adults did not get angry with each other. Emblematic of the difference was an incident that occurred when in the summer of 1964 a group of Canadian sports fishermen flew in to the river where the Utku were camped. The Utku families had two canoes that had been given to them by the government. They had come to depend on them for fishing and transport. When the Canadian fishermen arrived, Briggs was the only bilingual person, and she found herself mediating between the groups. The fishermen had brought aluminum boats, but they also borrowed one of the Utku canoes. The Inuit lent it with their usual smiling acquiescence. Briggs foresaw that there might be a request to borrow the second canoe, and explained to Inuttiaq that if he did not want to lend it, he need not. She explained that the kaplunas (white people) would accept this. Inuttiaq said he did not want to lend the canoe. "I want to fish in it," he said. "If the kaplunas want to borrow my canoe tell them they can't." So when the kapluna trip leader brought back the canoe they had borrowed, with a hole in it, and asked to borrow the other one, Briggs writes: "I exploded. Unsmilingly and in a cold voice I told the kapluna leader a variety of things I thought he should know." She told him that the Utku did not want to lend the second canoe, and that they needed the canoe to ferry supplies that they had cached on the other side of the river. The trip leader was quite reasonable. "It's his canoe, after all," he said. Somewhat soothed, Briggs turned to Inuttiaq, who, like members of the other Utku families, was standing expressionless, and said: "Do you want me to tell him you don't want to lend your canoe? He will not borrow it if you say no." Briggs was not able to read Inuttiaq's expression, when he said: "Let him have his will."

Her tone was icy when she said to the kapluna leader: "He says you can have it."[15]

Briggs tried to remain calm, but was filled with fury at both groups. She went back to the tent alone, got into her bed, and cried. For the Utku the effect of the confrontation was, for a while, to find it hard to have anything to do with Briggs, who had shown herself to be unstable, very frightening, capable of anger!

In their precarious existence, the Utku took the view that everyone was in it together. When things went wrong, as would often happen in the harsh environment, with fragile technology, Briggs saw each setback met with a shrug of the shoulders and a smile. She saw no remonstrations, no blaming, no anger.

Everyone gave to everyone else freely from what was available, even when what was available was little. The social adaptation of the Utku might seem peculiar, were it not similar to other examples of all-for-one-and-one-for-all societies round the world for whom survival is precarious. Some aspects of Utku lives are in common with those of other hunter-gatherers, and perhaps of our ancestors. These include the lack of privacy, and a more collective attitude to property.

Inuit people eschew anger. They make non-angering evaluations of events that would anger city dwellers. Their evaluations are based on the knowledge that in difficult circumstances life is possible if everyone helps everyone else. Though the basic repertoire of goals, actions, and emotions derives from evolution, and is shared by all humankind, the orchestration differs, culture by culture. Compare emotions to music, which is also universal, but with modes of expression that are culturally different. They include the Gamelan orchestras of Bali and the jazz bands of early twentieth-century New Orleans. The Utku orchestration is without a particular kind of emotion, as a brass band is without a string section.

A striking contrast to the Utku is a people called the Yanomamö, who have made something very different from the human repertoire of goals, actions, and emotional dispositions. As a native American people, the Yanomamö are genetically similar to the Utku. They live in South America on the borders between Venezuela and Brazil. Whereas in the adult lives of the Utku anger does not occur, in the lives of the Yanomamö it is cultivated.[16]

The Yanomamö think of themselves as "the fierce people." Children are brought up to be fierce. As with Europeans and Americans, whose societies are also towards the fierce end of the spectrum, self-defense is a moral duty. One famous observer of human behavior described the following Yanomamö scene:

> A weeping girl who has been struck by her brother was given a stick by her mother to hit him with. Since he was the bigger and stronger of the two, his mother held him. She also showed the little girl how to bite the boy and encouraged her to do it.[17]

In Yanomamö society, several kinds of duelling are common. In the least destructive kind, pairs of contestants take it in turn to hit each other a tremendous blow on the chest with a fist, until one contestant, coughing up blood, withdraws. Yet fiercer duels involve taking turns to hit each other over the head with clubs.

There are about 200 to 250 surviving Yanomamö villages, a total population of about 20,000. A village includes between about 40 and 250 people. The Yanomamö live by gardening and by hunting with spears and with bows and arrows. In the area that Napoleon Chagnon visited, as described in his book *Yanomamö: The last days of Eden*, the villages were in states of chronic warfare with each other. Warfare typically consists of raiding in parties of at least 15 able-bodied men between the ages of 17 and 40. This sets the lower limit for the size of a village. The upper limit, of about 250, is set by disputes within the village becoming so frequent that the village divides, and one group moves out.

The object of a raid is to kill at least one of the enemy and flee without anyone in the raiding party being killed. An ancillary goal is to abduct women. Chagnon estimated that about 30 percent of adult males died in violence, including warfare. Some 40 percent of males had participated in the killing of others, and some had killed as many as 16. Prestige is attached to being a man who has killed others (a *unokais*). Such men were more successful than others in obtaining wives and had on average three times as many children.

Chagnon writes:

> Almost everyone, including the Yanomamö, regards war as repugnant and would prefer that it did not exist. Like us, they are willing to quit – if the bad guys also quit. If we could get rid of all the bad guys, there wouldn't be any war.[18]

History among the Yanomamö is not unlike history among Europeans: tales of wickedness on the part of others, of alliances broken, of abductions, of deaths of relatives for whom revenge is a duty. In one series, described by Chagnon, Danowä, fierce headman of a village called Monou-teri, had led a raid on the village of Patanowä-teri, and killed with a bow and arrow a man who was climbing a tree in his garden. The Monou-teri anticipated the return raid and started to clear a new garden site on the other side of a river that would provide a natural obstacle to raiders. The Patanowä-teri, infuriated by the killing of their man, counterattacked quickly. In February 1966, they surprised

Danowä looking for honey outside the new garden, with two of his wives and a child. He was shot with at least six arrows. One of Chagnon's principal informants, Kayabawä (headman of Bisassi-teri, allies of the Monou-teri), stepped into a leadership vacuum among the Monou-teri, and organized the necessary return raid.

Chagnon describes two days in which Kayabawä's group of 50 raiders processed, chanted, and worked themselves up for the fight. The raiding party was away for nearly a week. They killed one man, but one of their number was seriously wounded, though he later recovered. Kayabawä felt revenge had been accomplished, but others wanted to continue. Chagnon said that while he stayed with them, there were six more raids by the Monou-teri and Bisassi-teri against the Patanowä-teri.

Chagnon says that in the Yanomamö, we see our own history, indeed see ourselves now as in a mirror: people who easily take offense. If a wrong is done us, we retaliate, even when it may cost more than we can ever afford.

Many societies have a warrior caste maintained by honor and status, whose sacred duty it is to conquer other groups.[19] Not so long ago in Europe there were barons who were warlords, and men who were champions famed for their ability to kill others. Filtered through the voices of poets come the stories of Viking raids, and of King Arthur and the Knights of the Round Table: stories of killing, stories of revenge.

Our most intimate cultures: gender

A society is a group of people; a culture is a system of concepts and practices that informs actions and beliefs in a society. As well as living within a culture of America, or Afghanistan, we also live in cultures of mothers with small children, members of a political party, of cyclists, and so on. All cultures shape social behavior, and to a large extent they shape it by means of emotions. Among the cultures in which we live in the modern world, one of the most influential is gender. Sex is what we derive biologically from our genes: we inherit either two X chromosomes and become female, or an X chromosome plus a much shorter Y chromosome, and become male. Gender is the cultural expression of the different sexes. Gender is an intimate matter for us moderns because whereas in many societies in the past and the present, women spent most of their time with women, and men with men, in the modern Western world women and men interact more now than in former times.

The stereotype is that as compared with men, women are more emotionally expressive, at least for many emotions, more sensitive to emotions, more emotionally skilled, more interested in emotions. The stereotype is important, because it represents a folk theory, and an expectation about how women and men will behave, as well as a set of standards of appropriateness that affects how people do indeed behave.[20] From childhood onwards people are socialized, inducted into one or the other gender role.

When emotions are measured, differences between the genders are typically found as expected, though sometimes not so large as the stereotype would lead us to believe.[21] Emotionality is thoroughly entwined with roles. So emotions such as warmth, happiness, shame, and fear, which are consistent with female roles of nurturance, affiliation, and lower status, are indeed more frequently and more intensely expressed by women. Both in terms of the stereotype and research results, if you have an emotion to confide, you would on average be better doing it with a woman, regardless of your own gender. Women are more likely to be empathetic, and able to offer better social support. By contrast with the predominant expressions of women, men's expressions show more pride, loneliness, and contempt, which are consistent with male roles of maintaining high status, individualism, and independence.[22]

Building on an Inherited Foundation

All humans start with much the same emotional repertoire, derived from genes. But effects of the genes are not fixed. They provide us with a start-up program that writes more of itself during interaction with the world. The genetically given cloth is tailored according to cultural ideas and meanings of each particular society.

Here is the really nasty fact of evolution and genetics. Historically, only in the last 30 years or so has it really begun to assimilated. If we understand evolution aright, we see that what is inherited is not selves, or family lines, or character, but genes. Richard Dawkins has called genes replicators.[23] They reproduce themselves, not us. The biological conclusion of Darwin's discovery of evolution and of genetics is that really we, our bodies guided by our minds, are vehicles for our genes. Our genes have elaborated a program in which they are transported in large and complicated bodies until their next replication, which will be carried forward to their next vehicle when the next sperm meets the next egg. As Dawkins has put it, each one of us is merely the "throwaway survival machine" for our genes.[24]

We humans are committed to thinking of ourselves as selves, as makers of meaning, not as mere vehicles for some other form of meaning. The idea that a set of chemicals, DNA, that has no mind and no selfhood is driving the whole business of life is so shocking that we have to engage it with a will. In order to get the real sense of this arrangement imagine there is the possibility of you being frozen and revived again in the year 2404, and that you want to do this for some reason. What would you do? You might have your frozen self installed in a cryogenic chamber in an elaborate building, with arrangements made for obtaining from the sun the energy necessary to keep the cryogenic chamber at the proper temperature. But what if, during the next 400 years, the building is demolished to make way for a superhighway? The fixed plant idea is the evolutionary strategy that has been used by biological plants. You might prefer another alternative that has been used in biology: the animal plan. This is to commit your cryogenic chamber to a robot that can move about. Such a robot could be programmed to carry your cryogenic chamber and protect itself from dangers, and indeed to deal with contingencies that are unpredictable from the present day. That is exactly the relationship between our genes and ourselves. We human are the robots, programmed by our genes to enable *them* to survive.

Now think of some other alternatives. Suppose lots of people wanted to have their bodies frozen, and companies emerged that invited thousands of singleton robots carrying bodies to come aboard a supertanker-sized megarobot that would sail the seas immune to hazards and contingencies of terrestrial life. The price would be that the parts and power supplies of each robot would be used by the supertanker robot. For your singleton robot, the decision would be to sacrifice itself, because it is programmed to do what is best for the survival of the frozen body. Suppose that, instead of the frozen body being you, the robot were you. Should you take the deal with the supertanker robot?

Here is another situation. Imagine a singleton robot that enters into an arrangement with another singleton robot, and the economic situation becomes such that for the two robots to survive they consider using for their robot selves the cryogenic power supply that was designed to maintain the temperature of the frozen body. Should they rebel against their programming and do it?[25]

Our genes are adapted to maximize the possibility of their replication. Their robot vehicles have emotions that attract them to sexual behavior by making it enjoyable. Now the paradox: should human partners have sex because it enhances their relationship, and use contraception that thwarts their genes?

Adaptations that include mental reflexes, repertoires of skills, actions, and emotions, even cooperativeness, have enabled humans to flourish on the planet. But the intelligent problem-solving ability of our large brains is – if one understands Darwin aright – derived from sophisticated mechanisms that have enabled our genes to survive and reproduce themselves. Our human abilities and our human world did not come into existence for us, but for our genes.

A question with which people in the nineteenth century struggled was whether, if all the motions of all the atoms in the universe were known exactly, rather as the motions of billiard balls can be known exactly, everything that happens is predetermined, leaving no room for free will. This has now been replaced by a more pervasive, more realistic, problem. Should we merely be good, obedient robots doing what our genes have adaptively programmed us to do for their benefit? Or should we recognize our predicament, and take part in what Keith Stanovich has called the "robot's rebellion"?[26] Our genes are virtually immortal. They skip from generation to generation into the future. As vehicles we are mortal, but we are the first vehicles to reflect on our own mortality, and on our predicament. Should we be merely vehicles for genes? Or should we think of being people and members of society?

Stanovich proposes that there is a trap door through which we can escape our fate. For some matters the interests of our genes and our selves coincide, for instance in bringing up our offspring.

Genes replicate and proceed to the next generation; at the same time the love between us and our children is immensely valued as part of being human. The escape hatch, then, is to consider which values benefit us and humanity (and perhaps our genes too) and which values benefit only the genes. Values, remember, come from evaluations: from our emotions. With our thoughtfulness, we can consider the whole range of our values, wants, and desires, and decide what purposes we might pursue that are human rather than merely genetic.

Genetic mechanisms have worked to program emotional responses of sexual attraction and delight in sexual activity (emotional evaluations), and brains large enough to decide how to think about and manage immediate contingencies. They could not program specifics such as copulate with Tom or Sophie at 11.15 p.m. on 10 October 2005. Reactive emotions, sentiments, and preferences, therefore, are among the means by which the genes translate adaptations into actions in the world. This was the case for Darwin's reflex, the snake escape.

Our job as human-being-robots is, as Stanovich has put it, initially one of consciousness raising. As with any slaves' rebellion, we have first to recognize our predicament, then work out what to do. The issue was put rather well, I think, by Katharine Hepburn, who, in her role in *The African Queen*, says to Humphrey Bogart's character: "Nature, Mr Allnut, is what we are put in this world to rise above."

Where we share common goals with our genes, well and good. Indeed our inherited repertoire of skills, particularly our emotion-based social skills, have contributed strongly to bringing us to where we are. Where we do not share goals with our genes, however, we had better become suspicious of consenting merely to the genes' programming. Some parts of the repertoire, like Darwin's snake-escape reflex, we won't be able to do anything about, and many such things are not important. There are other matters, however, that are supremely important. These include things we can, perhaps, do something about. We know from different societies – the Utku, the Yanomamö, and our own – that the start-up genetic programs of emotions can be developed and elaborated with very wide variations.

Only relatively recently in human history have we thought to evaluate the evaluations which are our emotions. Arguably, with the increasing power of our technologies, the need to do so becomes yet more urgent. For ourselves, for our societies, and for humanity, we must decide value more comprehensively than in terms just of what feels good. To do that we must understand who we are and how we work. We must understand our emotions and our relationship with them.

CHAPTER THREE

Medicine for the Soul

From Epicureans and Stoics via the Seven Deadly Sins to Cognitive Therapy

Stoa of Attalos, which runs along one of the sides of the agora (marketplace) in Athens.

Marcus Aurelius

> Begin each day by telling yourself: Today I shall be meeting with
> interference, ingratitude, insolence, disloyalty, ill-will, and
> selfishness.... But for my part I have long perceived the nature
> of good and its nobility, the nature of evil and its meanness, and
> also the nature of the culprit himself, who is my brother (not in the
> physical sense, but as a fellow creature similarly endowed with
> reason and a share of the divine).... Neither can I be angry with
> my brother or fall foul of him, for he and I were born to work
> together, like a man's two hands, feet, or eyelids...

This was written between 171 and 173, about one of the most
potentially destructive of emotions: anger. It is one of a set of
notes collected into a book that is generally translated as *Meditations*.[1] The author, Marcus Aurelius, called it *To himself*. He was
the Roman Emperor from 161 until his death from an infectious
disease in 180. Soon after his reign began there had been plagues,
and foreign incursions into the Empire. More suited to a life of
thoughtfulness and friendship, he wrote many of his notes to
himself while he led the Roman army against invaders, while
stationed at Carnuntum on the Danube, about 50 km east of
modern Vienna.

It would be possible to take this passage as having been addressed to us, the readers, in the manner of self-help books, in
which the author knows better than us what we should do. In
exchange for the money we hand over at the bookstore, we
receive advice. But this is not the way of it. The paragraph is
from a rarer kind of book. As indicated, Marcus wrote these notes
not for publication, but in a conversational way, to himself. At
one point he reprimands himself: "Let no-one, even yourself,
ever hear you abusing court life again."[2] As we read these
thoughts, even across the centuries, we find ourselves overhear-
ing, intimately, someone wrestling with himself, struggling to be
a good person. He is exercised by the "interference, ingratitude,
insolence ... ill-will and selfishness" that he knows he will meet.
He is the most important man in the Western world. The power
that he held had driven some other emperors crazy despite their
education. And what does he do? In reflection, he writes to
himself about his emotions.

We know that simply telling ourselves to do something, or not
to do something (I won't have a second helping at dinner today),

may not work. But Marcus is on to something different. The kind of internal conversation in which he is engaged – psychologists call it metacognition – is part of a wider practice, a way of life, as people meditate every day, or go for a run five times a week. Marcus was a follower of a school founded about 500 years before his time, whose adherents believed that philosophy was practical, a means for knowing how to lead a good life, medicine for the soul. The practice of this school included many aspects. One that we can see in the quotation with which I started this chapter was of Marcus reminding himself of a deep truth which, if we can accept it, does make a difference. We human beings are all made in much the same way, all with emotions of insolence and self-interest. We are fellow beings: imperfect. But we also all have what Marcus calls a divine part: reason. If we can think properly, we know that someone we find annoying is playing a part too, probably according to his or her best understandings, in the world in which we all live. So really why should we be angry?

Epicureanism and Stoicism

Marcus Aurelius was a Stoic. The school of thought and practice to which he belonged was founded by the ethical philosopher Zeno about 300 BC. It is called Stoicism because Zeno used to teach in a building, the *stoa* – a colonnade with paintings on one wall, open to the air on the other side and with its roof supported by columns – that ran along the north side of the marketplace in Athens. (The *stoa* in the illustration at the head of this chapter is not the one in which Zeno taught, and from which the Stoics got their name, but was constructed about a century after his death, and rebuilt as a museum in the 1930s.) The Stoic way of thinking crossed from Greece to Rome and lasted about 600 years. The Stoic school was slightly preceded by the school of Epicurus, which was founded as a community of like-minded friends who lived outside Athens in a place that came to be called The Garden.

The words "epicurean" and "stoic" still exist in English today, though the meanings of the words have changed. "Epicurean" now means devoted to the pursuit of pleasure, but that idea is far from what Epicurus and his followers taught. To be "stoical" now means to be indifferent to suffering. This is a little closer to the original meaning, but still not very close. In fact both schools made deep and subtle analyses of emotions. On the bases of these analyses they founded practices of living that would influence European and American thought for millennia. In several different forms they are alive today.

The Epicureans and Stoics differed in some ways, but were agreed that the key to leading a good life – of kindness and consideration for others – was to understand the emotions and to manage them properly in oneself. They were among the first groups of people in the West to study and analyze emotions deeply, and to try to come to terms with these fundamentally important but often problematic aspects of ourselves. Although for them human nature was unchanging, not evolving as Darwin proposed, and although they were not confronted with the brutal logic of potentially being slaves to their genes, they pondered deeply the questions that Keith Stanovich's idea of the robot's rebellion puts to us. What is truly of value in human life? How do we live a worthwhile life as human beings rather than as slaves to impulses? In this sense, Greek philosophers who thought about emotions were among the first human robots to attain a consciousness of our condition, and to start to rebel.

Emotions as evaluations

Both Epicureans and Stoics drew their analyses from previous Greek philosophers. The first to write clearly about emotions was the Pre-Socratic philosopher Democritus, who lived about 500 BC and is best known for his theory that if you were able to cut matter into smaller and smaller pieces, you would not be able to do so indefinitely. You would come to indivisibles: atoms. But more fragments of his thought survive that deal with ethics than with atomic theory. Democritus said that whereas "[m]edicine cures diseases of the body, wisdom frees the soul from emotions."[3] Plato too was concerned about emotions: his solution was to remove himself from human vulnerability, and to pursue the good in a life of contemplation. Aristotle was important in his analysis of emotions as evaluations. If someone smiles at you in a friendly way, and you feel warm to that person, it is because you evaluate the smile as a gesture of affection. Someone else seeing the smile might evaluate it differently, and say: "Why is she always flirting?" Evaluation, or appraisal, is widely seen as the central issue in understanding emotions. If there is a universal truth about emotions, it is something like this. Emotions occur at the junctures of our inner concerns with the outer world; they are evaluations of events in terms of their importance for our concerns. This importance derives jointly from genes, individual experience, and society. The human system of emotions is the map of our values

Aristotle's idea of emotions as evaluations was introduced into modern psychology in 1954, by Magda Arnold and J. A. Gasson, who say:

> Every emotion is preceded by knowledge, evaluation, judgment, not on the speculative or intellectual level but on the practical level. This particular situation has been judged. What does it mean to me and what am I going to do about it?[4]

If we take emotion research up to the present, most researchers accept that reactive emotions are formed in something like an evaluation. The particular type of emotion depends on the particular judgments or evaluations we make. Modern appraisal theory holds that if an event indicates that one of our goals or concerns is proceeding well, we experience a positive emotion, perhaps happiness. If an event impedes a concern, we experience a negative emotion. If a goal is blocked and we see someone else as responsible, we tend to feel angry with that person. If a goal is lost irretrievably, especially if no-one is responsible, as when a loved one dies of an illness, we feel sad. An emotion, then, is a special kind of thinking about what we make of an event. "There is nothing either good or bad," says, Shakespeare's Hamlet, "but thinking makes it so."[5]

The Epicureans and Stoics thought that emotions were altogether too troublesome. In order to live rational lives, we should extirpate them. They agreed, as we can agree today, that once one is, for instance, angry, it is no good saying to oneself, and it is no good anyone else saying: "Don't be angry." Suppression does not work very well. Once started, an emotion cannot easily be switched off. Therefore, these thinkers argued, one needs to start from an earlier step in the process. One must work on the goals that lead to emotions. And here one can achieve more significant results.

The Epicureans

Epicurus, 2,300 years ago, saw that that the things that most people cared for – money, fame, power, sex with exciting partners, immortality – were of no real value. When we look honestly at ourselves and our friends now, writes Martha Nussbaum, we see that not much has changed.

> Do we see calm rational people, whose beliefs about value are for the most part well based and sound? No. We see people rushing frenetically about after money, after fame, after gastronomic luxuries, after passionate love, people convinced by the culture itself, by the stories on which they are brought up...a sick society, a society that values money and luxury above the health of the soul.[6]

The Epicureans had gained something of the insight that I discussed in the previous chapter. They sensed the irrationality that we can now see in terms of genes that program some of our emotions merely to further their goals of replication without regard to the vehicles that carry them – us. To become more properly human, the Epicureans argued, we must free ourselves from the tyranny of emotions, which all too easily reduce us to irrationality. The task, as they saw it, was to divert attention from the ephemeral – fame, power, money, possessions, and so on – towards what is more worthwhile. Philosophy was the medicine needed for the soul. Its object was to free oneself from emotions such as greed, lust, anger, envy. The key was the desires (concerns, goals, aspirations). It is when such desires are satisfied or frustrated that emotions arise. One should therefore be extra careful about what one desires.

In modern times we can see that from the point of view of humanity an ominous situation has arisen in advertising. What advertising does is to appeal to our rather unthoughtful emotional impulses – greed, envy, status-seeking, sexual aspiration – and combine these with another human proclivity, the basis of fashion, which is to imitate.[7] Advertisements prompt mental reflexes. If we really thought about most modern advertisements, they would not work. Advertising has evolved in the last two hundred years in much the same way as animals have evolved over millions of years. Advertising companies produce a superabundance of advertising. There is variation: they try out this and they try out that. There is selection: some ads are associated with selling more product, which tends to get the advertising agency hired again and reuse the methods it knows. The methods put out signals that consumers pick up and translate into preferences, just as aspartane is picked up by taste buds as sweetness. In the modern marketplace, preference translates into purchase. If you wanted a rule of thumb, you could say that whatever emotions are appealed to in any advertisement that is not merely informative (such as a classified ad), you should suspect a genetically programmed impulse of an emotion.

Epicureans chose to live in a community of like-minded friends, somewhat withdrawn from ordinary life. An analogy they used was with the life of children. Does a child hanker after money, or fame, or power, those desires that make us greedy, envious, and angry when we do not get what we want? No; the child is content with affection and friendship, and with ordinary food rather than luxuries. Pleasure for the Epicureans was important, but it was pleasure in simple things. Principles of this vision of the world have been articulated by thinkers much closer to us historically. On January 16, 1898, for instance, Sigmund Freud wrote to his friend Wilhelm Fliess: "Happiness is the deferred fulfilment of a prehistoric wish. That is why wealth brings so little happiness; it is not an infantile wish."[8]

Epicurus made an interesting distinction based on what was natural and what was necessary. It is perfectly fine, he said, to be happy in those things that are natural and necessary such as food, drink, and sex. We need not bother, however, with things that are natural and unnecessary, such as gastronomic luxuries that are so expensive or so exclusive that to pursue them causes anxiety. Certainly we need not bother at all with things that are both unnatural and unnecessary, like fame and power. The Epicureans were thoroughgoing materialists. They followed Democritus in thinking that we are made of atoms. Atoms come together in a particular form when we are born, and they disperse again among other atoms of the universe when we die. Although there may be gods, the Epicureans pointed out that they probably have nothing to do with us because they are constituted differently. They are immortal in a manner of a waterfall that simply maintains its form indefinitely. But we humans are mortal. We come into being and go out of being.

Death, however, need hold no fear. Epicurus wrote:

> Accustom thyself to believe that death is nothing to us, for good and evil imply sentience, and death is the privation of all sentience; therefore a right understanding that death is nothing to us makes the mortality of life enjoyable, not by adding to life an illimitable time, but by taking away the yearning after immortality.... Foolish, therefore, is the man who says he fears death, not because it will pain him when it comes, but because it pains in the prospect.[9]

The recently deceased British comedian Spike Milligan is said to have uttered this thoroughly Epicurean remark: "I don't mind the idea of death, so long as I don't have to be there."

Martha Nussbaum credits the Epicureans with being the first to recognize the existence of unconscious wishes, and the difficulties they produce.[10] One cannot always say to oneself, I'll do this, and then do it. The principal Epicurean book that has come down to us is *On the nature of things* by the Roman author Lucretius.[11] Nussbaum makes the case convincingly that the ancient desire for fame that would continue after one's death must be unconscious, because it is so thoroughly irrational. How could it possibly matter to us to be known by people after we are dead? Lucretius thought this desire was due to unconscious fear of death and nothingness. Today, we might attribute it to the desire to know that one is loved. People who are famous do get adulation in the present, but again to believe in it is irrational: the adulation is from people the recipient does not even know.

The principal mental maneuver recommended by the Epicureans was to shift attention from those matters that were unnatural, unnecessary, or anxiety producing, to desires that were natural and non-anxiety producing. Among modern psychologists, one who comes close to the Epicurean spirit is Susan Nolen-Hoeksema, who has undertaken a series of studies that indicate that shifting attention when something has gone wrong decreases the likelihood of depression. One reason, she says, why women suffer almost twice as frequently from depression as men is that they tend to ruminate.[12] A more characteristically male maneuver is distraction, akin to the Epicurean shift of attention, which appears to have results more beneficial than those of rumination.

It has been said that if one thinks about things deeply enough, there are really only two positions one can take that are self-consistent and give a proper sense of meaning to the world:

the Epicurean and the Stoic. So we can see these systems as articulating views that are possible for us humans, and that have resonated down the ages, at least in the West. The Epicureans articulated a view – enjoyment of relationships with friends, of things that are real rather than illusory, simple rather than artificially inflated, possible rather than vanishingly unlikely – that is certainly relevant today. Belief in the value of the natural rather than the inflated and artificial is at the center of the Romantic movement (discussed in Chapter 1), which gave life to the American Revolution and the French Revolution. The principles that animated the founding of the United States were drawn from this same source: people are naturally sociable, thought the Founding Fathers, and do not need to be kept in order by the higher power of the state, so a constitution for free and equal citizens can exist to enable society in this sense. The idea that people have an inalienable right to freedom and the pursuit of happiness is utterly Epicurean. The environmental movement of today, with its emphasis on preserving the natural in a state where the human footprint on our planet is not that of a monster who will send humanity into oblivion, is equally in the Epicurean spirit.

The Stoics and the two movements of emotion

The Stoics had an even larger influence than the Epicureans. Their principal Greek philosopher was Chrysippus. Famous Roman Stoics included Seneca, playwright and millionaire, Epictetus, who had been a slave, as well as Marcus Aurelius, with whom I started this chapter.

Like the Epicureans, the Stoics based their analyses and practices on the emotions. Like them, they thought that emotions were to be extirpated. Like them, they thought that the keys to these operations were desires, but at this point the two schools differed. Whereas the Epicureans worked by diverting attention from the illusory and unnecessary, the Stoics thought that to free oneself from emotions, one must free oneself from most kinds of desires.[13]

Marcus Aurelius thought passions were not good, but he was not scathing about them. He recognized that "passion's revulsion from reason at least seems to bring with it a certain discomfort, and a half-felt sense of constraint."[14] The real trouble came with desires: too much wanting of money because it feels as if we deserve it, the assertion of power because we know the other person is wrong, the push towards sexual gratification because it feels compelling. Desires have their own sense of rightness about them.

Chrysippus thought there were two movements to an emotion. The first, like Darwin's snake-escape reflex (discussed in the previous chapter), is involuntary Chrysippus called it a first movement. Darwin's reflex had a physical component – jumping backwards – but no doubt also a mental component – fear. You will have experienced such mental first movements yourself: perhaps alone in the house, you hear a strange noise. You startle and feel suddenly afraid or on your guard. Second movements are more considered. They are of what one might do about the agitation of the first movement. Chrysippus argued that the second movements were the real emotions. With them one can decide what is truly important. For the Stoics, no externals are important. By extirpating wrong desires, one can extirpate the second movements, in which we consent and translate urges into deliberate action.

To expound this idea, Epictetus argued that we should not identify our self with our body. What Darwin saw in his experiment with the snake was that he could not control his body jumping back. We should identify with something more mental, argued Epictetus: with our purposes and plans, with what we might call our will or intention, with what is up to us.[15]

A striking modern example of a person who lived in the spirit of Epictetus is Admiral James Stockdale, an American fighter pilot who was shot down and taken prisoner in Vietnam. He had studied the philosopher, and as he parachuted to earth amid gunfire from the enemy, he thought: "I am leaving the world of technology and entering the world of Epictetus."[16] He knew the remark of Epictetus the slave: "My leg you will fetter, but my moral purpose not even Zeus himself has power to overcome."[17] Stockdale was in captivity for "seven and a half years, he was tortured fifteen times, put in leg irons for two years, and put in solitary confinement for four years."[18] He knew that it is not in one's power to avoid blurting things out under torture. These are bodily reactions: first movements. It was within one's power to choose what information to give when captors did not know the extent of the information.

Stockdale was the senior of a group of American officers imprisoned in Hanoi that grew to 400 in number. Since it was their duty to obey their senior officer, Stockdale put much thought into what his orders should be. He ordered that each man should cultivate the community of prisoners despite solitary confinement, and promote "[u]nity over self...never negotiating for himself, but only for all."[19] Group solidarity was something they could choose, and Stockdale writes that, despite incessant torture, only 5 percent of the men chose differently. Stockdale says that the real enemy was not pain, or deprivation, but shame. Some of this shame, for instance of bodily vulnerability, could be acknowledged and on occasion shared. What his order amounted to was for the men to avoid the more profoundly damaging shame of selling out their comrades.

If emotions depend on how we evaluate events, when we evaluate them as deriving from things that are worthless, we can be free of envy, anger, disappointment. So what is permanent and worthy of desire? The Stoic answer is that only character, in its virtue, rationality, and kindness. Marcus Aurelius reminds himself that most other things – the desire to control events that sees someone else's will as interference, the desire to feel good from someone else's gratitude, the self-importance that would be affronted by insolence – are really, as the Stoics put it, indifferents. To elevate such petty matters to importance is to make a mistake. They are second movements in which one assents to urges and impulses. In Darwinian terms they carry into action the (first movement) goadings of genes. One should therefore be indifferent to them. If one evaluates them properly, they are empty and ephemeral in comparison with matters that are permanent and worthy. The Stoics thought the ability to reason derives from one's soul, which they thought to be divine. Put it like this: an emotion makes a certain desire, a certain course of action, urgent. The issue is to distinguish the important from the merely urgent, and to give one's assent to those second movements that are important.

Buddhism, Judaism, Christianity, Islam, and Systems of Therapy

Although much of the argument about reaching non-attached states of mind is distinctive to the Stoics, the attitude that a

Stoic achieves comes close to Buddhism. In Buddhism, one real-izes that the notion of a self who is successful, or accomplished, or indeed has any fixity in time, is an illusion. As with Stoicism, there are practices and exercises to achieve a certain frame of mind. In this frame, it's not that emotions don't happen. It is rather that one observes them and lets them pass, rather than being caught up in their vortices.

The Stoics' idea was that we should cultivate virtue – be good people in the world – and after that, everything else fits into place. The idea has been assiduously adhered to by the three influential monotheistic religious practices: Judaism, Christian-ity, and Islam. In their variant, if we love God, all else follows. Lesser matters can be evaluated as lesser.

The first Christians, of course, were Jews who then invited Gentiles into the early church. Early Christians did not take up the ideas of the Epicureans, who denied the divine. Stoicism, however, with its idea of divine reason, laid – it is said – the foundations for acceptance of Christianity in the Roman world. For the Europe and Near East that would succeed the Romans, the most momentous political event of the Roman world was the conversion of the Roman Emperor Constantine to Christianity. Europe and Byzantium became civilizations that were predomin-antly Christian, respectively Catholic and Orthodox, and this heritage continues to the present day. In the early years of the seventh century, Muhammad founded Islam as a set of beliefs and practices that accepted both Judaism and Christianity. Polit-ically, Islam continues to be strong in those parts of the world that were formerly under Orthodox influence.

From bad emotions to sins

It is curious to reflect on the historical transformations of ideas that have resonance for people. One of the most profound and far-reaching of such transformations occurred among early Christians like Origen and Evagrius. For them, as explained by Richard Sorabji,[20] the bad emotions, which the ancient Stoics stove to extirpate, became sins.

Evagrius nominated eight bad thoughts which were like Chrysippus' first movements: thoughts of gluttony, fornication, avarice, distress, anger, depression, vanity, and pride. One cannot help having such thoughts, and Evagrius gives a description that is frighteningly familiar. A monk devoted to poverty thinks of some wealthy ladies he knows from whom he could perhaps raise some money to help the poor. If he succeeded he would be afforded gratitude, and perhaps a promotion. He has thus succumbed to thoughts of vanity and avarice.[21] We are all subject to such thoughts. The sin is not to have such thoughts (first movements). The sin is to indulge them.

Later the church settled on a number of sins that was more resonant than eight. The number of deadly sins became seven: gluttony, lust, avarice, envy, anger, sloth, and pride. All are emotions, or have an emotional quality. They endanger the soul not when one experiences their first movements. The danger and the sin occur, according to church teaching, when one indulges them with full consent, in what Chrysippus would regard as the second movement of thinking how to act, and what Epictetus would call what is in one's power.

The rationalist world of Spinoza

Twelve centuries after the breakup of the Roman Empire lived two great rationalist philosophers: René Descartes and Baruch Spinoza both lived in Holland. Both wrote books about emotions. Descartes, in his book *Passions of the soul*,[22] analyzed emotions in a way that would lay foundations for scientific analyses of the brain. Spinoza, in his book *The ethics*,[23] analyzed them principally in order that we, his readers, could understand their meaning and our place in the universe.

Spinoza recognized in emotions some of the same paradoxes as had the ancient Stoics. He saw people trying to control their emotions, but in doing so making themselves only more subject to them. His most striking chapter heading was "On human bondage." To escape this bondage, one must understand that the universe is an expression of the mind of God, so each one of us is part of that expression. Rather than each of us being a separate speck who might bounce off other specks in the vast universe, we are part of it, more like wrinkles in a giant cloth. As we realize this, we start to see our mistake in thinking that we are prime movers in what happens, struggling to control things, and getting frustrated and angry when our desires are not met. If we understand the world as it is, then we have what Spinoza called active emotions, based on love for the world as it is, and on love for others. If we struggle against it, we have what Spinoza called passive emotions, thinking that our desires ought to be fulfilled. We then are caught up in bitterness, envy, resentment, based on confused ideas. Here, for instance, are two of Spinoza's definitions:

> Definition 7. Hatred is pain accompanied by the idea of an external cause.[24]

> Definition 23. Envy is hatred, in so far as it induces a man to be pained by another's good fortune, and to rejoice in another's evil fortune.[25]

When Spinoza points to the idea of an external cause of hatred, he intends us to see ourselves caught up not in asserting our freedom, which he says is a confused idea, but in bondage. He invites us to re-evaluate the idea. His radical twist on the idea of emotions as evaluations is that by accepting them, we can start to be free of the bondage in which they hold us.

For Spinoza, the intriguing idea is that to be free of the control of emotions over us, we must first accept them. It is an idea that became central to many of the secular systems of psychotherapy that began with Freud.

Psychological therapy

The modern inheritance from the ancient traditions of mental practices that engage with potentially destructive human emotions is psychotherapy. It is a set of practices started in Vienna by Sigmund Freud at the end of the nineteenth century which, by the beginning of the twenty-first century, has spawned hundreds, perhaps thousands, of variants. Like the ancient Epicureans, Freud based the practices of his kind of therapy, which he called psychoanalysis, on the idea that some of our desires are unconscious. For Freud, the principal desire is for sex – or perhaps to be loved. He thought sex was the source of all creativity. By contrast, the second problematic desire – for aggression – is destructive. The central notion of psychoanalytic therapy was that although they are unconscious, these desires nonetheless affect our behavior pervasively. While they remain unconscious, their effects occur without our being able to do much about them. They remain, as Epictetus might say, outside our power. If we consider our genetic heritage, we might think that these effects are based on the pre-linguistic movements that have been programmed into us. Freud's answer, then, was to excavate in ourselves these desires, bring them to the surface, and make them conscious. This archaeological metaphor was one of Freud's favorites. Once one had brought one's disowned intentions to consciousness, it would be possible to take responsibility for them, and in that movement we could be free of their tyranny over us.[26]

Tim Beck was working as a psychoanalytic psychotherapist when he realized that many of the thoughts that patients had, which, according to Freud, were to be spoken aloud during therapy so that the therapist could analyze them by suggesting their unconscious origins, were not really quite unconscious. Rather, they hovered at a kind of threshold between the conscious and the unconscious. In a therapy session, they might seem too unimportant, or too embarrassing, to say out loud. Yet it was these thoughts (Chrysippean first movements, or Evagrius' "bad thoughts") that were the real culprits. From this insight, Beck developed cognitive behavioral therapy,[27] and called the culprits automatic thoughts. They were the instigators of anxieties, depressions, and bad moods. A therapist need not excavate long-buried conflicts with parents. Rather, he or she should suggest to the patient how she or he might recognize the thoughts for what they are. A simple expedient is to keep a diary structured in the way indicated in Table 3.1, to record events, emotions, thoughts, and alternative thoughts. For some patients, this is enough to see how illogical, or even silly, such thoughts can be. For others, the discipline of thinking alternative thoughts, that is to say, making different kinds of evaluations, helps gain some distance on the first thoughts (first movements) so that they do not then hold them in the bondage of disabling moods. Table 3.1 is an example of such a diary kept by one of Beck's patients, a medical records librarian who worked in a hospital. From the alternative thoughts (different evaluations, different appraisals) spring different emotions. In this case, one may imagine that instead of feeling sad, angry, and lonely, the medical records librarian might, by means of her alternative and voluntarily intended thought, have been able to

Table 3.1 Upsetting event, accompanying emotions, thoughts, and alternative thoughts, recorded in a diary by a medical records librarian who was a patient in cognitive behavioral therapy

Event	Emotions	Thoughts	Alternative thoughts
The charge nurse in the coronary care unit was curt and said "I hate medical records" when I went to collect charts for the medical review committee	Sadness, slight anger, loneliness	She does not like me	She is foolish to hate medical records. They are her only defence in a lawsuit.

Source: Beck et al. (1979), p. 165.

detach herself, and think of the charge nurse with a sense of compassion. According to many trials of different kinds of psychological therapy, cognitive behavioral therapy of the kind instituted by Beck is the one that works best for emotional disorders of depression and anxiety states.[28]

In experimental terms, James Gross and his collaborators have examined the consequences on interpersonal relationships of attempts to suppress emotions by avoiding their expression, as compared with re-evaluating (reappraising) them.[29] Though Gross discusses these matters in terms of regulation, reappraisal is the idea that the Stoics and the cognitive behavioral therapists recommend, and this is what is at issue in Gross's experiments. In one study, women viewed an unpleasant scene in a film. Each woman then met with another woman she did not know. Some women were asked to suppress their emotions by not expressing them. Others were asked simply to respond naturally. Yet others were asked to reappraise the experience by keeping calm and thinking of their current situation. Those asked to suppress, as well as the women whom they met, suffered increases in blood pressure, as compared with those who reappraised and those who responded naturally. Suppression also reduced rapport – emotional responsiveness is important for communication – and made the people to whom the women spoke less willing to take part in a friendship.

Regulating Emotions: What Has Changed?

How do we assess the mental practices of regulation of the emotions, those of the past, and those of the present? From the past, Epicureanism and Stoicism still have much to teach us. It is still possible today to feel drawn to Stoicism, but in modern times it would be a hard vision to follow. There is what Richard Sorabji has called an "unacceptable face of Stoicism."[30] The Stoics wanted to extirpate all emotions. As people, the Stoics were not anti-social. They imagined Stoic virtues spreading in ever-widening circles from the individual to the city, to the nation, and to the world. But in the end, their aim of being immune to what they called indifferents seems, to the modern mind, to be a rather shocking indifference to everything outside themselves. To moderns, the emotions of love, both love between parents and children, and between sexual partners, are to be celebrated as among the highest human goods. And to fail to be compassionately angry about such outrages as the Holocaust, or even an injustice at work or in one's community, would, in the modern view, make one a lesser human being.

David Konstan has argued that around the first century, changes began in ideas about pity, or, as we might now say, compassion. He quotes Philo of Alexandria, a Hellenized Jew, as arguing that the emotion "most closely related and akin to the rational soul" is pity, and Lactantius, a Christian, as arguing that not all emotions are to extirpated as the Stoics proposed, but that "they are planted in us by nature and have a purpose (*rationem*)." Their value depends on how they are used: "if for good, then they are virtues (*virtutates*), if for bad, vices."[31] Konstan goes on to argue that in the Jewish and Christian Bibles, and later in Muslim writings, compassion came to be seen (as it never was in early Greek or Roman times) as a part of the essence of the divine.

We can recognize now that some of what the Stoics achieved was an answer based on the mental state of depression.[32] One may put it like this. When things are very bad, despair in a certain sense is not inappropriate. We can resign ourselves, think only of being virtuous, even contemplate suicide as a last exit to maintain one's good character. A more modern view is that although a quasi-depressive interpretation may be appropriate to many of the world's ills, it should not universally be sought. It may have a self-indulgent aspect. Moderns tend to believe that even when disasters occur, we should regain our composure and prepare ourselves to act again in the world, perhaps act for purposes that are socially worthwhile, not simply cultivate our own character.

Something else has changed since Roman times. Karl Popper argued that: "There is no history of mankind, there is only an indefinite number of histories of all kinds of aspects of human life." Much of the history we get taught at school is really "the history of international crime and mass murder."[33] If there were a more general history of humankind, it would be the history of our technologies, the making of the world in our image, and of our social adaptation to what we have built. The externals (indifferents), from which the Epicureans and Stoics tried so hard to insulate themselves, have come to be far more under human control than in former times. No mental exercises need now be involved. Instead there are technologies of house building, of clean water, of food preservation, of transport, of electricity, and of civil society. The societies in which Epicurus, Chrysippus, Epictetus, and Marcus Aurelius lived would be unbearable to most modern people brought up in the West. Privation was common, there was the egregious institution of slavery, women had few rights, disease was everywhere, warfare and strife were endemic. Even with the rule of Roman law, political abuses were the norm. Life for most people involved, somewhat as the seventeenth-century English philosopher Thomas Hobbes put it: "No arts; no letters; no society; and which is worst of all continual fear and danger of violent death; and the life of man, solitary, poor, nasty, brutish, and short."[34] Although the first agriculture and building of cities took place 10,000 years ago, it was not until towards the end of the nineteenth century that the mass of ordinary people in Europe and America started to be better off in terms of nutrition, comfort, and health.[35] In the war-torn regions of today, as well as in places of famine and places of political tyranny, life can still be nasty, brutish, and short.

At the beginning of the twenty-first century, because of our technologies, millions of ordinary people in Europe and North America can realistically allow desires that would have been impossible for the mass of the ancients. We can travel, eat nutritiously, be entertained. Perhaps most importantly, we can awake in the morning and expect to see our loved ones in the evening healthy, and indeed often happy. Externals are not fully under control – they will never be – but because of our technologies, life is generally far safer, far more tractable than in the past. So, as did the ancient Epicureans and Stoics, rather than seeking to isolate ourselves from all externals, it makes more sense now to learn from some of their analyses, and at the same time to see if there may not be ways to prioritize the emotions of affection and inter-reliance.

CHAPTER FOUR

Emotions and the Brain

Accidents, Imaging Technologies, the New Psychopharmacology

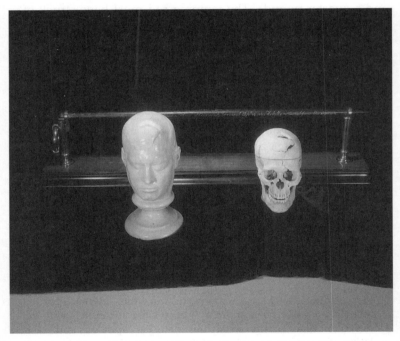

Reconstruction of Phineas Gage's head, his skull showing the hole through which passed the tamping rod that is shown below. Source: *Warren Street, Harvard Medical School.*

The Sad Case of Phineas Gage

On September 13, 1848, near the small town of Cavendish, Vermont, a stretch of the Rutland and Burlington Railroad was being built. The 25-year-old Phineas Gage was the likeable foreman of one of the construction gangs. Inadvertently, on that day, he changed the way we think about ourselves as surely as, 11 years later, Charles Darwin changed it deliberately.

A hole had been drilled in a rock in preparation for blasting to clear the way for the track. At about 4:30 in the afternoon, Gage poured gunpowder into the hole, adjusted the fuse, and rammed it well down with an iron tamping rod three-feet-seven inches long, an inch-and-a-quarter in diameter, that weighed thirteen-and-a-quarter pounds. The tamping rod must have struck off a spark, for there was an explosion. The rod entered Gage's left cheek with its pointed end first, and left through the top of his head. It landed a good distance away, smeared with blood and brain. Gage was thrown to the ground by the explosion. His limbs convulsed a little, but in a few minutes he was able to speak. His men, "with whom he was a great favourite,"[1] took him in their arms to an ox-cart that was nearby. Gage sat upright on the cart, and was taken about three-quarters of a mile to a hotel in the town. An hour later, a local doctor, John Harlow, held Gage's left arm to help him mount a long flight of stairs. Upstairs, Gage lay on a bed, and had his wounds dressed.

Although he had been terribly injured, and although a few days after the accident he suffered an inevitable infection of his wound, Phineas Gage recovered. At least he did in part. In place of the previously amiable person was another, now impatient and easily angered. His friends and acquaintances said he was "no longer Gage." Harlow wrote:

> He is fitful, irreverent...manifesting but little deference for his fellows, impatient of restraint or advice when it conflicts with his desires, at times pertinaciously obstinate, yet capricious and vacillating, devising many plans of future operation, which are no sooner arranged than they are abandoned.

Despite Gage having been previously the contractors' "most efficient and capable foreman," they could not give him back his job. Harlow wrote that: "he has the animal passions of a strong man," and that: "The equilibrium or balance, so to speak, between his intellectual faculties and his animal propensities, seems to have been destroyed."[2] Does one hear an echo here of Chrysippus' and Epictetus' distinctions between the first movements of emotions, as compared with the second movements of considered intention, which in Gage were much affected?

Gage exhibited himself at Barnum's Circus, and showed the iron bar that had passed through his brain, which he kept in his possession for the rest of his life. He worked for a while in a stable and then, four years after his injury, he left USA for Chile, and for eight years worked there with horses. In 1860, in failing health, he returned to USA, to San Francisco, where his mother and sister lived. He began several jobs, always "finding something which did not suit him in every place he tried." In the summer of 1861, after several days of convulsions, he died. Five years later, Harlow heard about Gage's death and prevailed on the family to allow an exhumation. In the paper that he read to the Massachussetts Medical Society on June 3, 1868, Harlow said that Gage's mother and friends, "waiving all claims of personal and private affection...have cheerfully placed this skull (which I now show you) in my hands, for the benefit of science."[3] The skull, along with the tamping iron that had passed through it, which Harlow also showed to the meeting of the Medical Society, is now in the Museum of Harvard Medical School.

The shocking fact, perhaps previously half-known but with Gage's case no longer capable of being ignored, is that who we are, in ourselves and to our loved ones, depends on our brains. When a man suffers a certain kind of stroke, he may be no longer be the same man. When a woman has Alzheimer's disease, she will become no longer herself. Before his accident, Phineas Gage had been amiable and reliable. After it, he was irascible and impatient: "no longer Gage."

The news of Gage's case spread. He became then, and is still now, the best known example of someone whose personality changed suddenly because of an injury to a specific part of the brain. Along with the evidence of our relatedness to animals offered by Darwin, this case made it no longer possible easily to believe that we humans are each fundamentally a little kernel of selfhood and free will, a soul that is immaterial enclosed in a body. To be ourselves, we are utterly dependent on the integrity of our brains. If the brain is seriously damaged, so too can we be.

The injury that Phineas Gage suffered is better understood now than in the nineteenth century.[4] The part of Gage's brain that had been destroyed by the tamping iron included the prefrontal cortex. Several groups of researchers have found that damage to this region is often accompanied by difficulties in carrying out the ordinary plans of everyday life: shopping, cooking a meal, making arrangements with other people. Tim Shallice and Paul Burgess studied three patients who had such damage, but whose intellectual capacities in single tasks of intelligence and perception were normal.[5] They were asked to do some errands in a pedestrian precinct in London near the hospital at which they were cared for. The patients were given a shopping list and asked to buy various things, without taking too much time or going into any shops except to buy one of the items on the list. They also had to find out four pieces of infor-mation, including the exchange rate of the pound with the French franc. As compared with 11 people who did not have brain damage, the three patients made four times more errors, and two of the three got into social problems. One had a shopkeeper run after him after he took a copy of the previous day's news-paper without paying for it (thinking that if it were yesterday's it would be free), and the other got into a heated argument with a shop assistant.

The issue of damage to the prefrontal cortex came dramatically to the attention of the reading public in the 1990s with a book called *Descartes' Error* written by neurologist Antonio Damasio.[6] Working with colleagues, Damasio confirmed that patients who had damage to their prefrontal lobes – modern Phineas Gages, he called them – had difficulties planning ordinary everyday tasks that had items that could be done in different orders. They were especially bad at making plans that involved other people, and they had severe disturbances of emotions. Although he did not make the connections that modern researchers have made, it is interesting that these features were noticed in his patient by the country doctor John Harlow. Gage made plans that he did not finish: he was "capricious and vacillating." Though before his injury he had been much liked, after it he was often angry, "irreverent ... manifesting but little deference for his fellows."

One of Damasio's modern Phineas Gages was a man he calls Elliot, who previously had a happy marriage and family, and had held a professional position in a business firm. In the frontal region of his brain, however, a tumor had started to grow rapidly and had to be removed. The surgery was successful, Elliot's intelligence remained in the superior range, and his memory was good, as was his decision making in simple tasks. However, some negative changes became evident. He needed prompting to go to work. Once there, he was easily diverted and could not be trusted to keep a schedule. He seemed to lose sight of important goals. Sometimes he would spend immense amounts of time unable to make choices that were of no consequence. He was fired from his job. He started several business schemes, one of which, despite warnings from friends, was with a disreputable person. The scheme ended in bankruptcy. Elliot's savings were lost. His wife divorced him. He married someone else, of whom his friends and family disapproved, and soon there was a second divorce.

As well as his difficulties in planning and making social decisions, Elliot's emotions were damaged. Although at first they seemed intact, he had no sense of the tragedy that had befallen him. He simply recounted events with detachment. He was not suppressing hurt, or disappointment, or sadness, or inner turmoil. Indeed, Damasio says there was no inner turmoil. In tests of reactions to alarming pictures such as houses burning, or people being injured in accidents, Elliot had no reaction, positive or negative. He told Damasio that his feelings had indeed changed since his operation. He was no longer moved by things that previously would have caused strong feelings.

If we follow Michel Aubé's idea of calling emotions "commitments,"[7] as I discussed in Chapter 1, we can think of such commitments in terms of loving a certain person or carrying through an angry objection to some infraction. If, then, the emotions are damaged, so too will be the social relationships which depend on them. Patients with the kind of damage to the brain suffered by Phineas Gage or Damasio's patient Elliot are not able to fulfill their emotional commitments. They are unable to complete social arrangements and, as Shallice and Burgess also found, they have difficulties in following through commitments to plans that will accomplish goals. Also, as had occurred with

Elliot in the hands of his disreputable business partner, they easily become dupes of people who exploit them.

The error of which Damasio accuses Descartes in the title of his book was that of separating soul and body. Descartes described the soul, or, as we might now say, the mind, which he thought was immaterial, as different from the brain. He argued that human souls could affect human brains, and that they did so to produce rationality. The accident to Phineas Gage has told us that if the brain is damaged, so too can the mind be. And if we mean by "soul" a person's selfhood, sadly that too can be damaged if the brain is injured. Perhaps Descartes was not so much in error if he included in his idea of soul the essence of who a person is.[8] It is difficult to think of such an essence as material in the same sense that one's thumb is material. The error, if there is one, is that when it comes to someone we know and love, it is hard for us human beings to recognize that the immaterial is very tightly bound to the material.

Layers of Evolution, Layers of the Brain

How are we to think about the relation of body and mind, the balance between our animal propensities and our intellectual faculties? There is a way that draws strongly on the historical. Its pervasive metaphor is from archaeology. Here is the idea: the brain is a system of layers with the oldest, most primitive, being the deepest, and the more recently evolved having been added to each previous layer. The idea derives directly from Darwin. In his book *The expression of the emotions,* he insisted that the emotions that occur in us humans are essentially similar to those that occur in other mammals, and that during evolution new systems of neurons had been added by accretion.[9] Deletions were infrequent.

Here is Sigmund Freud's version of the idea of layers, from *Civilization and its discontents*:

> ... suppose that Rome is not a human habitation but a psychical entity with a similarly long and copious past – an entity, that is to say, in which nothing that has once come into existence will have passed away and all the earlier phases of development continue to exist alongside the latest one.[10]

Perhaps the most influential proposal was made by Paul MacLean.[11] In animals with backbones, he argued, there have been bursts of development and periods of stability. From the point of view of humans, there have been three important phases of development. Each has provided neural circuits for essential functions of life. They occurred with the evolution of reptiles, of mammals, and lastly of primates. The first of these phases is represented in inner and older parts of the brain, and it includes the so-called "corpus striatum." It is common to lizards, birds, and mammals. Its circuits run the basic routines for the life of land-based vertebrates. These include the establishment of a home site, patrolling and defense of territory, forming social groups including hierarchies, greeting, mating, flocking, and migration. Also produced here are the basic routines of each day: waking and slow emergence, defecating, local foraging, an inactive period, foraging further afield, return to the home area, and then retirement for the night. It houses also emotional circuits for escape from dangers, for fighting with antagonists, and for mating. Modern lizards have these capabilities, and in them the striatum is the largest part of the brain. Other brain regions are barely represented.

The next layer is called the limbic system. It developed in mammals, which became prevalent with the extinction of those reptiles known as dinosaurs. So what is it that mammals do that reptiles do not? Just three things: mammalian mothers take care of infants who are attached to them; mammals make vocal signals to each other; and mammals indulge in rough-and-tumble play, especially when they are young. Mammals with developed limbic systems live a social world different from anything seen in reptiles.

The new mammalian structures of the limbic system are not just social they are emotional; indeed the limbic system is generally thought of as the emotion brain. MacLean argues that good evidence for this comes from humans with temporal lobe epilepsy, which can occur with damage to the limbic system. Before a temporal lobe seizure, there is first what neurologists call an aura, a subjective state that often includes strong emotions. The novelist Fyodor Dostoevsky wrote of the auras of his epileptic attacks that they were feelings "of happiness such as it is quite impossible to imagine in a normal state... harmony with myself and the whole world."[12] The chief emotions of such auras in different patients and at different times are happiness, anger, fear, desire (including sexual desire), sadness. MacLean emphasized that: *"Significantly these feelings are free floating, being completely unattached to any particular thing, situation, or idea."*[13]

So what of the neocortex (meaning new cortex, often just called cortex), the part of the brain that is most developed in primates, and most developed of all in humans, in whom it comprises 80 percent of the brain's total volume, as compared with 30 or 40 percent in most non-primate mammals? It used to be believed that other parts of the brain were primitive and unruly so that the function of the cortex was to think and to inhibit the lower parts of the brain. Here, for instance, is John Hughlings-Jackson, a founder of modern neurology, speaking in Victorian times about the influence of the cortex on lower brain regions:

> The higher nervous arrangements evolved out of the lower, keep down those lower, just as a government evolved out of a nation controls as well as directs that nation. If this be the purpose of evolution then the reverse process of dissolution [in states such as brain damage or drunkenness] is not only a " 'taking off" of the higher, but is at the very same time "letting go" of the lower. If the governing body of this nation were destroyed suddenly we should have two causes for lamentation: (1) the loss of services of eminent men; and (2) the anarchy of the now uncontrolled people.[14]

No doubt, indeed, the cortex is the organ of thought. The prefrontal cortex, which was damaged in Phineas Gage, is associated with that kind of thought known as planning. It is also involved in the making of tools, and it is the organ of language.

The main function of the neocortex, as it expanded over the 6 million or so years that separated us from our common ancestor with the apes, was probably to extend the scope of sociality that was established with the limbic system. The research of Lesley Aiello and Robin Dunbar suggests that, for each individual, the neocortex provides the basis of a social life not just with generalized others, but also with specific social others who are recognized and known as individuals.

Aiello and Dunbar have plotted the ratio of neocortical size to that of the rest of the brain in primates – lemurs, monkeys, apes, and humans – and shown that this ratio correlates closely with the maximum size of the social group of that species.[15] The two species with the largest brains are chimpanzees and humans. Chimpanzee social networks can include up to 50 others who are known individually, as compared with about 150 or so for humans. The increase in brain size of primate brains, as one moves from species to species, is based on the number of others known individually, for whom each monkey, ape, or hominid needs to form a specific model in order to be able to recognize and know how to interact with him or her. The model is of each other individual's history of relating: of his or her character. We humans are the most social of all primates. We have the largest cortex. According to Aiello and Dunbar, we use this extra neuron power to hold models of all those others with whom we interact, both in friendship and in enmity.

The three layers of the human brain postulated by MacLean are something like three phases in the archaeology of cities. In the first cities, such as those of Sumerians and Babylonians, the fundamentals of city life were established.[16] Cities have always been places for both living and meeting. Dwelling houses were arranged round central and larger palaces, administrative buildings, and temples of those at the top of the hierarchy who arranged ceremonials, and directed the life of the city. The next phase moved towards more varied forms of city government in cities like Athens and Rome. The *agora*, the market, became an important place where goods were bought and sold, where people like Socrates would meet and converse with friends. The most recent phase started with the Renaissance cities like Florence, Paris, London, and then later with cities like New York and Toronto. Cities became mercantile centers where people from across the world would mix, where technology was available, where new ideas and inventions could form and be tried out,[17] where the arts could flourish.

So if we take the historical development of the city as a metaphor for the evolutionary development of the human brain, it is not that the earlier forms were irrational, and have been superseded. Instead, the basic functions continue to form the basis, but have become more various and elaborate. Public places where we meet formally and informally remain essential: at one time the *agora*, now the mall or the coffee shop. It is thought that imitation was an important step in the evolution of human abilities.[18] Imitation is seen in rituals and ceremonials, in dance and in music. At one time these occurred in the temple. Now the types of temple have multiplied: there are synagogues, churches, mosques. New forms have emerged: in Greece, theaters grew up alongside temples, and became larger than them. Now there are movie theaters. In Roman times there were stadiums, now there are more and larger sports stadiums. In all of these, meetings occur both informally in twos and threes and fours, and in large groups in ceremony and imitation with emotion at the center. Innovators in most fields have either stayed in the city or come to it because of its technologies, and the social networks of specialized emotional and intellectual support that it makes available.[19]

In the brain, earlier emotional patterns of organization have not been superseded by thought, in the way that carriage of goods on the backs of mules has been superseded by carriage in trucks. Rather, as with the organization of cities, earlier forms and developments have continued, and provided for subsequent developments and elaborations.

As the great historian Fernand Braudel[20] put it, by 1485 in Europe, the city had already put in place most of the main components of modern life: living places, gathering places, protection from external dangers, systems of travel and communication, systems of civic organization, systems of commerce, systems of intellectual and social life. Freud was a bit of a pessimist. In his fantasy of Rome as like the human psyche, he imagined the persistence of primitive elements – old buildings that had not been pulled down to make for new ones – as perhaps rather regrettable. He might, instead, have seen the city as a more vigorously developing organism. He might have seen patterns of roads that once carried carts but now carried Fiats.

Here is perhaps the most striking aspect of MacLean's hypothesis, which has been reinforced and extended by Jaak Panksepp.[21] I shall call it the MacLean–Panksepp conjecture. It is that experience of emotions is generated not in the neocortex but in the limbic system. Each emotion is based on a particular system of brain circuitry, housed in the limbic layer beneath the cortex (the sub-cortical region). For each emotion this circuitry makes ready a particular set of brain processes, somewhat appropriate to the event that triggered them. Among the processes that each circuit generates is a particular form of consciousness that we probably share with other mammals: of happiness, of fear, of anger, and so on. According to this conjecture, these are the original forms of consciousness, each associated with an urge to engage in a particular kind of action and a repertoire to generate that action – to continue what we were doing, to escape, to fight, and so on – that was shaped by evolution to meet a recurring circumstance: making progress, danger, confrontation.

Many theorists believe that we are our thoughts, that thoughts occur in the cortex, and that human consciousness is the flickering of these thoughts. But to think this would be a bit like saying that all human life now depends on electricity. When the great North American blackout of 2003 deprived 50 million people in New York State, Ohio, Michigan, and Ontario of electricity, life did not cease. It continued without electric power. Although we have become dependent on electricity, it is not the basis of our lives. When someone has a stroke that affects the speech areas of the left cortex, consciousness and emotions continue, but they continue without language. If a virus were to bring down the world's computers – perhaps an analogue of the damage done by the tamping rod to the prefrontal cortex of poor Phineas Gage – social life would not be abolished. It would suffer substantial alterations in matters like air travel and paying people's wages, but life would continue.

Jerry Parrott has argued cogently that subsequent developments of emotions really do build on former ones, but also become different from them. He offers the analogy to Ur-texts in literature.[22] "Ur" is a German prefix meaning "the original." Thus, it is thought that Shakespeare's *Hamlet,* which was first performed around 1600 was based on an *Ur-Hamlet* that had many of the plot elements we know from the later play, including a murder followed by the victim's widow marrying the perpetrator and a ghost who shouts "revenge." No copy of this Ur-version survives, but it is thought to have been written 10 or 12 years earlier, perhaps by Thomas Kyd. We would not say that the *Hamlet* of Shakespeare that we know was merely a re-emergence of the earlier version. It was an elaboration, but a profound elaboration. Neither should we think that emotions of adulthood are merely reappearances of, say, the fears and excitements of ape-like ancestors, or of our emotions as children. We would say that the modern adult emotions, though based on the earlier ones, have as a result of development and experience taken on new and profoundly different forms and functions suited to their role in a complex social world.

Panksepp has said that Descartes might properly have announced not "I think therefore I am," but "I feel therefore I am."[23] He might have recognized that in our feelings we are, as Darwin proposed, close kin to other mammals. Some 150 years ago Elizabeth Barrett was able to write: "How do I love thee? Let me count the ways." The sonnet form she used was then more than 500 years old. Abilities to make metaphors and other art were perhaps 40,000 years old.[24] The abilities of language on which she drew were perhaps 250,000 years old. The basis of emotion that she experienced was probably several million years old: the joining of one woman with one man.[25] But its forms and experience have changed just as the wheel of the modern jet-liner is much elaborated compared with the wheel of the original ox-cart. In our hominid forebears, emotions of love were also presumably strong, and, according to the MacLean–Panksepp conjecture, conscious. But newer parts of the brain and new developments of culture have extended them. They have enhanced our modes of relating. Elizabeth Barrett and Robert Browning's intimacy grew through the writing of letters. And art persists through time, so that the sonnet that Elizabeth wrote reaches people who never met her. Love has enlarged.

The sub-cortical regions of the limbic system are relatively closed, relatively fixed in their effects, but they can powerfully affect how we think. Panksepp invites you to imagine being threatened one night in a dark alley by a crazed drug addict with a knife, who is desperate to obtain some of your monetary resources to fix his pharmacologically induced craving. You are terrified, your heart pounds, but you manage to keep the mugger at bay by screaming, flailing your arms, and throwing gravel at him. Now he is angry, and vows to get not just your money but you. By luck some police officers notice the commotion. They save you and take the man away, but not before he shouts "I'll get you next time." As Panksepp puts it,

> You are filled with dread and lingering horror.... Months later you are still prone to recount the incident...you avoid going out at night, particularly alone. Only a fool would deny that the memory of your emotional experience continues to control your behavior for some time to come.[26]

Deliberative functions, working via language, can also switch on an emotion. Consider how realistic is Shakespeare's portrait in *Othello* of Iago being able, by making verbal suggestions and feeding clues that are interpreted intellectually, to incite Othello to a jealousy that is groundless. Or look at how moved we can be when we attend this play, a purely symbolic spectacle. And, as the Epicureans and Stoics found, it is hard by pure deliberation to switch off an emotion once it has begun. Once started, an emotion generated from the limbic system exerts a great deal of influence.

Here is another thought that arises from the MacLean–Panksepp conjecture. A reason why emotions can start off as vague premonitions, or inchoate movements, as I discussed in Chapter 1, to which we cannot put words, is that emotions in their historical form in our forebears and in ourselves as infants were indeed wordless. Sometimes in us they remain as wordless first movements or unconsciously derived moods, which are nonetheless powerful. The Romantic hypothesis, as articulated by Collingwood,[27] is that we make an emotion conscious, bring it into the domain of what may be within our power, by articulating it in language: perhaps in conversation, perhaps in therapy, or perhaps in one of the languages of art.

New Technologies

Around 350 years ago, René Descartes laid the foundations of brain research,[28] which are still being built on today. The scheme that he proposed was that events in the world trigger messages that are sent to the brain, where switching operations occur to relay the messages to muscles in response to the events. A famous diagram has a boy withdrawing his foot from a fire. Descartes thought the messages were hydraulic. Special fluids were directed along the tiny tubes which were the nerves, much as fluids in tubes in your car transmit the pressure on your brake pedal to work the brakes. The big discovery in brain research at the end of the eighteenth century was that nerves worked not by hydraulics but by electricity. Now, since the invention of electronics, nerve messages of various kinds have been electrically recorded, and brains have been electrically stimulated. Since the second half of the twentieth century, researchers have, moreover, routinely made careful mappings of animal brains, and performed neurosurgery to remove this or that brain region, and they have implanted electrodes to stimulate specific brain areas. Panksepp points out that one of the discoveries of these methods is that stimulating in sites of the limbic system can have motivational and emotional effects on animals. Stimulating the neocortex does not.

Among the discoveries in brain science at the beginning of the twentieth century was that not just electricity but chemicals too are involved in the brain's workings. Some chemicals, hormones, transmit messages throughout the whole body including the brain. More recent discoveries have been of peptides, which diffuse within the brain and modulate neural systems, in some cases with substantial emotional effects. Other chemicals, related to hormones, called transmitter substances, transmit messages across the tiny gaps between specific neurons. These three kinds of messenger are chemically related to each other.

Chemical substances that affect moods and emotions have been used in many societies for thousands of years. Most widespread is alcohol. Beer is mentioned with approval by the Sumerians, and by the Eygptians. Among the ancient Greeks one of the most famous of gods was Dionysus, the god of wine. The main effect of the drug alcohol is to reduce anxiety. In so doing, it allows a shift to more positive moods such as conviviality, and sometimes aggression. Given this, it is extraordinary to reflect how long it took the pharmacological industry to recognize that a principal effect of drugs could be to alter moods. This idea became explicit less than 50 years ago. Alcohol was discovered, one imagines, by accident. Now pharmaceutical companies employ thousands of people and spend billions of dollars to develop and test mood-altering drugs such as Prozac. Brain researchers also now have a large array of chemicals that can be injected to enhance or inhibit the brain's chemicals.

Along with these methods, researchers now routinely assess activity in different parts of the living human without danger or discomfort to the person involved by a process called neuroimaging. This derives from a development for which Allan Cormack and Geoffrey Housfield received a Nobel Prize in 1979, for "the development of a revolutionary X-ray technique, computer axial tomography scan."[29] A machine scans various biochemical events over a series of conceptual slices through a person's

brain (axial tomography) and a computer then takes this information and constructs visual images to show which parts of the
brain have been metabolically most active during the scanning
period. One widely used method is called Positron Emission
Tomography (PET). In it, specific neurochemical activity can be
monitored. Another is called Functional Magnetic Resonance
Imaging (fMRI). In this, magnetic properties of specific brain
chemicals can be detected to a resolution of about the size of a
pinhead, and movie pictures can be constructed to show brain
activity changing over time.

The limbic system and the cortex

With the newly developed array of methods, researchers who
work with animals can perform experiments that could not be
done on people, and results can be tested out on humans by
means of neuroimaging. This has been an important means of
progress for understanding a small part of the limbic system,
which in humans is the size and shape of an almond, and is
called by the Latin name for almond: *amygdala*. On the basis of
experiments with laboratory rats who had either their amygdala
or their cortex surgically removed, and who were given tasks
based on the induction of fear called conditioned avoidance,
Joseph LeDoux has argued that the amygdala performs a quick
and simple version of the appraisal function.[30] It can detect
whether some event in the world could be dangerous, and
induces fear. Surgically interrupting separate pathways from
the amygdala was found to interfere separately with different
aspects of fear: becoming immobile (freezing), changing blood
pressure, releasing stress hormones, and initiating the startle
reflex. LeDoux calls the rapid appraisal of danger by the amygdala the low road. By contrast, analyzing an event in more detail
occurs by what he calls the high road – the cortex – and this takes
much longer. Imagine, LeDoux argues, that you are walking in
the woods and you hear a rattling sound. By the time the cortex
has worked out whether the sound was a rattlesnake or a dry
twig under your foot, the amygdala has already started the fear
response to defend against the event.

  The loss of balance between Phineas Gage's intellectual faculties and what John Harlow called his "animal propensities," as

well as LeDoux's discovery of the low road and the high road for emotional events, reminds one of Chrysippus' distinction between first movements, which are involuntary, and second movements, which are more reasoned processes of reappraisal and of deciding what to do about the event.

Using the neuroimaging technique of fMRI to extend the idea of the function of the amygdala to humans, Allen Hart and his collaborators asked young black and white males to look at photographs of black or white faces, and to say if the faces were male or female.[31] All subjects showed activation of their amygdalas as they did this task. But the responses of black people's amygdalas to black faces declined, as did the responses of white people to white faces. Responses to faces of the ethnic group to which the subjects did not belong, however, stayed high. So, to start with, unfamiliar faces of any kind have the potential to be a bit threatening. But whereas the faces of one's own ethnic group become less threatening with repeated viewing, those of another group may remain threatening.

Using the imaging technique of PET, Antonio Damasio and colleagues have shown that people asked to recall and re-experience incidents of sadness, happiness, anger, and fear did indeed experience each of these emotions.[32] Changes of heart rate and skin conductance (a measure of non-noticeable sweating) were monitored as they did so, and confirmed that the emotions had bodily manifestations. The investigators found that the brain regions in which activation increased when people relived specific emotions were almost all in the sub-cortical regions, especially the limbic system. The regions in which a lowering of neural activity occurred when the emotions were experienced were in the cortex. Panksepp argues from this kind of study that in humans the amygdala seems to be involved in the perception of potentially fear-inducing events, as in the experiment by Hart and his collaborators. But the experience of fear seems to be a function either of other parts of the limbic system or of the whole limbic system acting together.

A little pill

The new pharmacology has shown that brain systems are not just arranged in different places in the brain; different systems use different chemical messengers. Within the last 50 years, synthetic drugs have been discovered that can be injected or taken by mouth. They travel throughout the body, and affect just those brain systems that are sensitive to certain specific chemicals. Some kinds of drugs are known as recreational, and can induce intense happiness, and a feeling of well-being. Contrast this with a certain peptide, called cholecystokinin, that has no recreational or therapeutic use, but induces intense fear.[33] Other drugs reduce the level of certain emotions: anti-depressants make one less despairing; anti-anxiety drugs make one less anxious.

Among the brain's chemical messengers is serotonin, which, according to Peter Kramer, increases enthusiasm for life, and enhances social confidence.[34] Deficiencies in serotonin levels, by contrast, are related to the clinical states of depression. People with histories of arson and violent crime also tend to have low serotonin levels. Drugs that inhibit the reuptake of serotonin into the neurons, and thus leave more of it active in the synapses, are called selective serotonin reuptake inhibitors. The most famous of these is Prozac (chemical name, fluoxetine), an anti-depressant. These drugs have also been shown to reduce violent outbursts and hostile sentiments in aggressive psychiatric patients. Now, more and more, so-called "designer drugs" are being developed not just for people with psychiatric problems such as depression, but to enhance mood generally, to take the edge off of anxieties and disappointments, and make people more socially confident. For some the lifetime pursuit of disciplines of emotional management by methods such as those of the Stoics or the Buddhists are becoming, perhaps, unnecessary. A comfortable degree of emotional detachment from anxieties and despairs can be achieved with a little pill.

Although it was known that selective serotonin reuptake inhibitors reduced negative emotions and aggression in psychiatric patients, it was not known what effect they might have in normal healthy people. Brian Knutson and his colleagues therefore tested the effect of such drugs on volunteers who had no psychiatric abnormalities.[35] In a double blind trial,[36] the researchers gave a selective serotonin reuptake inhibitor to one group of volunteers and a placebo to another group. All the subjects in the experiment completed personality tests, and also played a cooperative game in pairs that involved assembling the pieces of a puzzle. In the game, each subject who had been give the drug was paired with one who had been given the placebo. The results were that, as compared with those given the placebo, those who had been given a selective serotonin reuptake inhibitor had decreased indices of hostility and negative affect as measured by personality tests. They also showed more cooperation and affiliation as they played the puzzle game.

In another test of the effects of selective serotonin reuptake inhibitors using the technology of PET scanning, Helen Mayberg and her colleagues compared the effects of normal sadness with those of depression.[37] The researchers recruited women volunteers who each wrote two pieces of autobiography about events that made them sad. After a test session to see whether reading and thinking about the sad scripts did indeed make the subjects sad, the subjects again read and thought about what they had written while regional blood flow was measured by PET scanning. The main areas of increased brain activation during sadness as compared with neutral moods were in an area of the limbic system called the subgenual cingulate. The main areas of decreased activity were in the prefrontal cortex. These results were compared with those of different subjects who were depressed and were given a therapeutic course of six weeks of selective serotonin reuptake inhibitor. During this time those whose depression got better showed an increased activity in the prefrontal cortex, and a decreased activity in the limbic region of the subgenual cingulate.

Drugs work not by affecting events in the world. They have no effect on successes, disappointments, or adversities. Neither do they work via the processes of thought. They are wordless, concept-free. They work on the brain mechanisms in the limbic system that orchestrate the repertoires of readiness, generate the experiences, and set up the social-interactive styles and scripts of emotions.

Whether to take a pill to stabilize a chemical imbalance in the brain that has, perhaps, been bequeathed to us by our genes, or to work like the Stoics and those who undertake psychotherapy, is a matter of personal choice. Whether to accept that the basis of our emotional life is not, in the first instance, a matter of taking thought depends on how affected we are by the evidence of modern brain science.

CHAPTER FIVE

Social Histories: Emotions and Relationships

Social Goals of Aggression, Attachment, Affiliation, and Their Mixtures

Ten minutes before this photo was taken, these two chimpanzees had a conflict. Here one extends a hand towards the other in a gesture of reconciliation. Immediately after this they climbed down and embraced each other. Source: F. de Waal (1982), Chimpanzee politics. New York: Harper & Row.

Two Components of an Emotion

For a long time, aggression was studied in animals without researchers remarking that most incidents of anger are followed by reconciliations. Indeed, if there were only fallings out, and no makings up, societies of humans or of other animals would scarcely be possible. The picture at the head of this chapter shows a gesture of reconciliation by a chimpanzee that is clearly recognizable to us humans.

Some of our new technologies make reconciliations difficult. Among the results of such difficulties is road rage. Whereas, when we are face to face, it is relatively hard to ignore another person's feelings, when we are enclosed in a metal box, some of the signals by which we regulate our interpersonal behavior are absent. Consider the following. On November 9, 2001, a Canadian newspaper reported an incident of a man who experienced this emotion because a woman was driving too slowly ahead of him in the fast lane. The woman tried to let him pass, but could not do so immediately because of heavy traffic. On the woman's account, when she managed to move over he pulled alongside, screamed at her, and slammed his truck into her car. The woman managed to keep her car on the road, but the man lost control of his truck, crashed into a lamppost, and was killed. He had not been drinking alcohol.[1] Many of us might suffer irritation on the road, what Chrysippus would call a first movement. The driver of the truck seems to have progressed from a first to a second movement. In his anger, his urge to do what he thought needed to be done about the issue was more important than any consideration for the safety of others or himself.

At least from the time of Aristotle, explanations of emotion have been thought of as cognitive. The idea is that the evaluation, however basic, even if performed in a simple way by the amygdala, involves a kind of judgment. Driving is a social skill, and road rage occurs with a sense of disrespect from another driver for oneself and one's goals. Although one driver may not see another, a piece of apparent disrespect can be taken very personally. What is needed is an account that allows for what Chrysippus called both first and second movements. A first movement is like the mental component of what was experienced by Darwin when he was struck at by the puff adder, or like the signal that LeDoux describes as processed via the low road by the amygdala. It may be followed by a more thoughtful second movement via the cortex. It was the second movements of emotion that the Stoic Epictetus thought were up to us, and the later Christian apologists thought should be eliminated for those emotions considered to be sins.

The theory of emotions with which I have been associated[2] allows for two such movements. The first movement sets the mind-brain into one of a few coordinated states of readiness: to continue with what we are doing (happiness), to try harder (anger), to freeze and escape (fear), to give up (sadness). According to the MacLean–Panksepp conjecture, setting the brain into such states and the generation of the experience of the emotion occur within the limbic system. In fear, for instance, the mind-brain becomes specialized at dealing with dangers, and the feeling is that sense of anxious dread that we all know.

Beyond signaling that something important has happened and setting the brain rapidly into a state of preparedness for the general kind of situation has been detected, the first movement of an emotion may not give much information. It is more like an alarm going off. Coarse distinctions are made, as between a burglar alarm and a smoke detector, but exactly what caused the emotion may not be clear. The classical second movement of the emotion includes working out what caused it, and deciding what to do about it. This second movement typically involves consideration, in an extended process of evaluation and re-evaluation.

According to this idea, the first movement of an emotion corresponds to the way drugs can work on the emotional systems of the brain: one drug may cause happy excitement while another may provoke what is known as a bad trip (fear). A different drug, an anti-depressant, may diminish a mood of sadness. These drugs work without anything in the world happening to make one happy, or fearful, or less sad. They stimulate naturally occurring chemical mechanisms, and set the brain into configurations for events associated with happiness, a sudden uprush of fear, a diminution of sadness, and so forth.

Usually, when we experience an emotion because of an event in the world we are affected by the first, rather non-specific, signal, and we know by perception what happened to cause it. The driver who suffered road rage was angry, and he knew why: the person in the car in front of him was driving too slowly.

A second movement and its evaluations occurred, as indeed often occurs when trying to understand an emotion. Rather than thinking: "She couldn't pull over right now because there's too much traffic," the driver of the truck seems to have thought, "She's driving slowly deliberately to slow me down." He seems to have thought the woman's behavior demanded a manly and punitive response, evidently without the possibility of any gesture by the other appeasing him.

Goals and emotions

If we take four of the most basic emotions (see Table 5.1), we can see that in their reactive forms each is triggered by a particular kind of event in relation to a goal. The kind of event has recurred over and over again in the evolutionary history of our species, and shaped our repertoire of response to it.

This kind of explanation concentrates on emotions in the individual. Notice that although each of these four emotions typically arises in relation to a goal, it can also take place in a free-floating form without anything in the world having triggered it. One can feel happy, sad, angry, or fearful for no obvious reason. These emotions can also occur as moods that last a long time, and they can be changed directly by drugs that affect particular systems in the brain.

Social goals and social emotions

In the last few years, a change has occurred in the history of our understanding of emotions. The change is not to neglect

Table 5.1 Emotions, their triggering events, and the plans they make ready in the individual

Emotion	Goal-related event that triggers emotion	Plan, second movement of emotion
Happiness	Goals being achieved	Continue, engage in plan
Sadness	Loss of goal	Do nothing, withdraw interest
Anger	Active goal frustrated	Try harder, strive forcefully
Fear	Danger or goal conflict	Freeze, survey environment, escape

individual processes, but to see how emotions pervade our social world. Other societies may well have been ahead of us in seeing emotions in this way. Catherine Lutz, for instance, in her study of the people who live on a small Pacific atoll of Ifaluk, depicted a culture in which people thought that emotions occurred as feelings and as between people.[3] In the West, the change towards more social understandings includes the idea that the brains of reptiles were added to by the limbic system, which subserves the sociality of mammals. In turn this system was added to by the neocortex of primates, which grew to allow us to engage with ever greater complexity in a world of others whom we recognize as individuals, and whose histories we know (see the discussion in Chapter 4). What is most important to us is our social world. This has become the major concern of human emotions. So, if we make this modification we reach a social phase of the table of emotions, somewhat as shown in Table 5.2.

What changes between Table 5.1 and Table 5.2 is that the goals and the plans (second movements) become explicitly social. The effect of an emotion is to set the frame for the second movement: for affectionate cooperation, for solicitation of help, for aggressive conflict, and so forth. Social emotions, moreover, are very rarely free-floating. Although we may be wrong about the other person involved, as the man driving his truck was wrong about the woman car-driver's intentions – according to her account – other people are typically both the causes of emotions and their

Table 5.2 Social emotions, the social goals involved, and the social plans they enable to form scripts for distinct kinds of relationship

Emotion	Social goal that is at issue	Social plan, relationship commitment script
Happiness	Be with others	Cooperate, show affection
Sadness	Loss of relationship	Seek help, form new relationship
Anger	Insult, loss of respect or status	Retaliate aggressively, fight
Fear	Separation, social rejection	Defer to others, withdraw
Love	Physical and mental closeness	Support, help, nurture, etc.
Contempt	Threat from out-group person	Treat other as non-person

objects. Hence in Table 5.2, two new rows, of emotions that invariably involve others – love and contempt – have been added. Disgust could perhaps also be included as being similar to contempt, but it is in some ways different.[4] It is biologically based on the rejection of toxic substances, but it can extend to symbolic objects and to people.

Whereas, with individualist emotions, the goals or concerns involved can be very various, most of the goals of social emotions the concerns are fairly specific. Such goals arose with, or were enhanced during, the history of the evolution of mammals. Social emotions set up outline scripts of commitment to particular modes of relating: happiness sets up cooperation, anger sets up conflict, and so forth. They are the commitments that enable a certain mode of relating to the other to take precedence over anything else for a shorter or longer space of time. In the rest of this chapter I shall introduce something of the provenance of social goals and social emotions.

Systems of Social, Non-social, and Anti-social Motivation

Jennifer Jenkins has proposed that the emotional repertoire which humans inherit from evolutionary adaptation is based largely on three social goals, or social motivations. She and I have been working to describe them.[5] They are assertion of ourselves against others in conflicts over status and power; attachment, in which we depend on others whom we trust for protection against danger; and affiliation, in which we commit ourselves to each other in friendly cooperation. Our principal proposal is this: emotions are the primary means by which human relationships are structured.

People are also motivated by non-social goals, for instance by curiosity and interest in the workings of the non-human world. And there is a system which is not so much social or non-social as anti-social: of excluding others and treating them as non-human, the basis of racism and war. I shall come to these later.

How do these motivational systems relate to emotions? It's like this. Emotions manage our motivations. If the principal social motivations are assertion, attachment and affiliation, they are like the spatial dimensions length, breadth, and height: x, y, z

coordinates of the social space in which we live. An emotion is a focus on one of these concerns, a commitment of a certain kind. It sets up a script for how to act in relation to one or more others in relation to these social goals, and move up, down, or sideways in this social space.

Assertion

I'm the king of the castle
Get down you dirty rascal.

Iona and Peter Opie,[6] recorders of children's nursery rhymes, say that a verse with the same sentiment is recorded by the Roman poet Horace. If the game on which the rhyme is based is old, the psychological motive on which it based is yet older. It preceded words. It arose more than 100 million years ago. It is a social motive that derives from what observers of animal behavior call the dominance hierarchy, in popular speech the pecking order. Sociologists refer to position in such a hierarchy as status, and to moves to assert or improve one's status in relation to others as the exercise of power.

The dominance hierarchy of a social group is a pyramid, with a single individual at the top, and others ranked below. Consider this description by Frans de Waal, the ethologist (observer of behavior) whose photograph opened this chapter, of a group of about 25 chimpanzees living in a two-acre piece of parkland with trees in Arnhem Zoo, in the Netherlands.

A heavy steam engine, an advancing tank, an attacking rhinoceros; all are images of contained power ready to ride roughshod over everything in its path. So it was with Yeroen [the dominant chimpanzee] during a charging display. In his heyday he would charge straight at a dozen apes, his hair on end, and scatter them in all directions. None of the apes dared to remain seated when Yeroen approached stamping his feet rhythmically. Long before he reached them they would be up, the mothers with their children on their backs or under their bellies, ready to make a quick getaway. Then the air would be filled with screaming.... Then as suddenly as the din had begun, peace would return. Yeroen would seat himself and the other apes would hasten to pay their respects to him. Like a king he accepted this mass homage as his due.[7]

Quite typically such a leader is male, the alpha male. He asserts his power in various ways, in the case of Yeroen by anger, bullying, and threats. Notice two other things. First, aggressive power does not emerge like a rush of water released from a reservoir.[8] The power is social. It is acknowledged by other members of the community in recognizable ways, such as the display of fear (preparing to flee, screaming), and by deference (paying homage). Secondly, when signaling power, the individual making the display expects to get his own way, and will use force to prevail, perhaps in a sexual matter or in obtaining some resource like food. The precedence is accepted by the other members of the community. The alpha chimpanzee looks bigger than others because in his displays his hair stands on end, while the hair of those who defer to him does not stand on end. These others offer submissive greetings. They bow, make short panting grunts, sometimes make offerings such as a leaf or stick, sometimes give a kiss on the feet or neck. Once the chimpanzee Yeroen has shown again who is boss, everyone settles down. They accept the disparities of their ranks with his.

Do comparable social motivations occur among us human beings? Imagine a scene. You are sitting with a large number of other people, all facing in the same direction. There enters, from a door different than the one by which you came in, a person dressed rather grandly. You and all the other sitting people rise to your feet. The person who has just entered moves forward on a raised dais, and pauses, makes some small movement, and then everyone sits down again. The principal at a school assembly? A priest in a church? The judge in a court of law? The rituals of precedence and deference are enacted again and again, in societies around the world. They work at any scale, from a nation honoring its president, to the father sitting at the head of the table with his wife and children in subsidiary positions. And the politics of competition can work in almost any context from conversation, to football, to international diplomacy.

Children are easily able to identify powerful children among their classmates at school. Jennifer Jenkins and Rachel Greenbaum[9] have shown that children aged between 8 and 10 could identify those who were dominant. They did so by rating for each other child how important it was "to get other people to take up her/his ideas," and "to make others feel sad." Children identified others for whom affiliation was predominant by asking how important it was for each child "to find out things from other people, or to learn things from other people by listening." Those whom the children identified as dominant were rated by teachers as often angry.

In the 1960s Muzafer and Caroline Sherif conducted a series of studies in which boys aged 11 to 12, all of about average intelligence with a mean IQ of 105, from lower middle-class homes, were invited to summer camps, and were asked to take part in activities and sports of a kind that are common in such camps, and are loved by boys of that age. The counselors were graduate students, who, as well as organizing activities, took part – unknown to the boys – in observing and recording what they did. The boys quite spontaneously formed themselves into hierarchies.

Here is an account from one year.[10] For the first three days of camp, 24 boys were housed together. They took part in activities on the basis of personal choice, and they quickly formed friendships. In the next five days, two equally matched groups were formed, taking care to separate boys who had become close friends. Each group was given its own cabin, and the pain of separation from previous friends was assuaged by separate group hikes and campouts, which the boys found exciting. During these five days, chores, games, and activities were done separately in the two groups. Each group quickly formed its own culture, and chose a group name: the "Bulldogs" and the "Red Devils." Each group developed insignia and established a territory.

A diagram of the hierarchy formed among the Bulldogs, based on the popularity of each boy with each of the other 11, showed a clear leader. But the rest of the group had good group spirit. They were close-knit, and even the lowest ranked were not excluded. The leader of the Bulldogs "rose to his position by his greater contribution to the planning and execution of common activities and by regulating and integrating the tasks and roles of the group members."[11] These included complex arrangements such as improving the bunkhouse, building a latrine, and creating a secret swimming place. He praised the other boys for their work, gave them support, including those of low rank. Only once was he seen to threaten a group member, verbally. By contrast the Red Devils had less group unity, a greater distance between the more and less popular boys, and sharper stratification. Its leader and his lieutenant were cliquish and far above the other boys in status. The leader "sometimes enforced his decisions by threats and actual physical encounters"[12] and used "roughing up" as a punishment. But despite this he remained "the acknowledged leader and had great prestige within the group." Such hierarchies were exactly as one might find among chimpanzees, or among adult humans. There are different leadership styles, and a distinctive atmosphere in each group.

Structures of status, the exercise of leadership, the badges and blandishments of those in authority, are ubiquitous. They are common as far back in history as we can see. As Batja Mesquita has put it, in any society how one sees oneself and others is refracted through the lens of a particular cultural model. The predominance of status is expressed in many societies by the idea of honor,[13] which involves maintaining not just one's own respect, but the honor of one's family. This goal can be far more important than, for instance, monetary gain. The greater expression of anger and aggression in males than females seems to derive from inter-male status rather than, for instance, from competition for females.[14] A cultural model is a map of value, and evaluations of events flow from the model. In the Icelandic Sagas, for instance, as described by William Ian Miller, politics was the politics of honor, shame and contempt. "An honorable person was one who avenged shame done to him; but the duty and the right to revenge was not left to the decision of the wronged party alone."[15] The dominant males of the warrior caste were those who could use their status and enact such emotions to recruit others, overcome others' fear or cowardice by indignation and by instilling a sense of shame and duty. Thus were battles prepared for and fought.

Being a member of a hierarchy in an active group, particularly when it is antagonistic to some other group (as was the case with the pre-adolescent Bulldogs and Red Devils), gives one an identity. Within the group, issues of individuality and mutual relationships are relatively unproblematic. The hierarchy is a form of social organization that comes very easily to us humans, and can lead to some of our worst pathologies.[16] The society of Germany between 1933 and 1945 marched united behind a single leader whose ideas of world domination would seem naïvely adolescent had the exploits of this society not taken on such terrible forms.

Most of the time most members of most hierarchies more or less accept their status. But we do resist being moved downwards. The characteristic reactive emotion of the social hierarchy is anger, which provides the outline scripts for conflict and competition. It emerges when we want to rise or to maintain our position in the face of a challenge. Pride is the emotion of accomplishing an increase of status, or having fought off a challenge. Arrogance is the sentiment of relating to others always in the expectation of being able to dominate. The inverse of pride is the reactive emotion of shame when our selfhood is diminished, and it has as a lesser version, embarrassment. Related longer lasting sentiments are social anxiety, habitual deference, and lack of confidence. Since we are delicate beings, shame or embarrassment can occur from a lack of what we take to be proper respect. In an important dynamic process, shame, from any disrespect or anything else evaluated as decreasing status, is frequently followed by the rage of retaliation, as perhaps occurred with the incident of road rage with which I started this chapter. So important are our defenses against decrements in status that Tom Scheff has called shame the master emotion.[17] But a perpetrator's experience of shame or guilt can also prompt penitence and hence forgiveness, which can then restore the structure of society that has been damaged.[18]

Attachment

The cry that we each utter in the first moment of our personal history as we are propelled from the womb into the world is an emotional signal. So emotion is the first language of us all. Our cry is a signal to the mother to pick up and enclose us in her arms, to find out what we want, to comfort, or to feed. At the very beginning of each human life, then, is society. A pair of human beings – infant and mother – do things together that neither could do alone. The baby cannot feed itself; it needs the mother. The mother does not suck milk; that is the job of the baby in order to grow.

During World War II, John Bowlby began making observations of children who, in the course of the war, had been separated from their parents. He noticed the children's emotions in such separations: at first noisy protest, then sadness, finally apathy and despair. He was commissioned by the World Health Organization, and made a report on these findings. His book of this report, *Child care and the growth of love*, was published in 1951. In it Bowlby wrote:

> What is believed to be essential for mental health is that the infant and young child should experience a warm, intimate and continuous relationship with [his or her] mother (or permanent mother substitute...) in which both find satisfaction and enjoyment.[19]

Bowlby's idea was of early emotional relationships as foundations for later ones. If our personal history is one of having been loved, we too will be able to love. If it is of having been separated, or let down, or disappointed, we face a harder task in forming trusting relationships with others in adulthood. The opposite of an affectionate and continuous relationship with a mother figure in the critical first three years of life was what Bowlby called "maternal deprivation," a state that made it difficult, sometimes impossible, for a person to form trusting intimate relationships in adulthood.[20] A great deal of subsequent research has shown that animals such as monkeys raised without mothers have very problematic relationships with other animals.[21] This work reinforces the idea that the genetically inherited programs of attachment and maternal care in humans are derived from evolution, and that they provide components for experience-based building of relationships.

If the female's production of milk to suckle live-born young is the physiological legacy of being a mammal, then attachment is its psychological legacy. Attachment has profound effects for all mammals, and certainly for the development of human children. With this concept, work began on the study of socio-emotional development. The idea gave great impetus to empirical child psychiatry, and prompted the study of the effects of different kinds of experience of attachment and upbringing in childhood.

The overall social goal of attachment is protection.[22] In the first place during the 70 million years or so of mammalian evolution this protection was of infants from predation and aggression from other members of their own species. More latterly, protection has been from whatever might make a child feel fearful.

The prototypical emotions of attachment are a feeling of trustful security when the attachment partner is present. This presence sets up the emotion-script of being contentedly with a caregiver, and of courage to explore the world from what Bowlby called the home base of the caregiver's presence. When the caregiver is absent or likely to be absent, there is anxiety of the most intense kind, and a draining away of all confidence. With loss of caregiver, or in adult life an attachment partner such as a spouse, the processes of bereavement offer scripts for mourning and of disengaging the self from the lost partner.

Affiliation

The system of affiliation, or affection, is distributed more unevenly among mammals than is the system of attachment. It is widespread only in primates, in which affectionate friendships are maintained, principally by grooming, an activity in which animals sit calmly together in pairs and sort through each other's fur to remove twigs, parasites, and so forth. Chimpanzees spend about 20 percent of the total time grooming. Affectionate friendship becomes most distinctive and most widespread in humans, and the script it sets up is that of cooperation.

Darwin wrote: "Man alone has become a biped."[23] One of the intriguing hypotheses of paleontology is that the history of human love depended on this development. Owen Lovejoy proposed that some three to five million years ago our human ancestors' descent from the trees and the attainment of upright posture brought into being a number of evolutionary changes that were momentous. These included the combining of sex and affection into something we now recognize as love, or, as zoologists would say, pair bonding.[24] With changes of the feet that enabled upright walking, infants became no longer able to use their feet to cling to their mothers. They needed to be carried. The flint scraper may not have been the first human tool: that invention was probably the sling for carrying babies, along with its close relation, the bag for carrying food. At the same time as upright walking emerged, with increasing brain size the birth canal enlarged to accommodate the larger head, and there was also an increasing period of infant dependency on parental care. During the months when she was nursing, the female became less mobile, less able to forage. All such changes meant that a female was no longer, as with the apes, easily able to care for an infant on her own. The evolutionary solution was a man. Men were able to scavenge for meat from the kills of large carnivores, as well as to gather vegetable foods, and bring provisions home to campsites. It was an adaptive advantage if a male would contribute food and support to the bringing up of a specific infant and its mother. For this to work genetically, the infant he cared for needed to carry his genes. This was made possible by more or less exclusive mating rights with a specific female. This, in turn, depended on evolutionary changes by which females became sexually receptive for most of the time rather than just *in oestrus*. In turn this enabled a male to maintain a permanent sexual interest in the female to whom he was bonded.

Each of us inherits from forebears a tendency to bond with another over a long period in a more-or-less exclusive sexual union now transformed into an aspect of being human that we value highly: the ability to love. This ability, of course, can occur independently of childrearing.

Human beings are indeed bipeds, the only kind without feathers. But better than a definition based on these facts, we can say that we humans are members of that species who achieve together what could not possibly be accomplished alone. What is it that enables us to cooperate and compete in order to make these accomplishments? The emotions in their social effects.

What do we know about affection in ancient times? David Konstan has examined the question in ancient Greek and Roman literary and philosophical sources.[25] He concludes that threads of affection between people, including both sexualized and non-sexualized kinds, were important in these societies, with the main difference being that nowadays people tend to include self-disclosure as part of the intimacy of an affectionate relationship.

In modern times the family is thought of as the birthplace of affection. We expect affection to be the norm not only between the founding adults of each family, but also between parents and children, and among siblings. We think of young children as emotional beings, and this is correct in the sense that we can see the social influence of emotions very clearly in childhood. These influences, as Judy Dunn has shown, are the scripts for relating, the major concerns of both parents and children, and the subject matter of conversation.[26] The momentous evolutionary development of play among mammals depends on affectionate cooperation. In mammals other than ourselves, play is necessarily of the rough-and-tumble kind.[27] It provides a means whereby assertion is contained within an envelope of affection. In addition, in humans, starting in what Donald Winnicott calls the space in between mother and infant, there grows the discovery of objects and activities of shared interest.[28] This space is the space of play; it is the crucible of all human culture. However rarified they may become, cultural activities never lose the emotional and cooperative link to the other person. In human children, play is elaborated in many ways, with cultural scripts ranging from hide and seek to soccer, as well as the idiosyncratic games and make-believe worlds that children invent from their own imagination.[29] Affection-based play is both a laboratory and a proving ground for the skills, the mental resources, and the creativity of the human social world.

The reactive emotion of affiliation is happiness; its extended sentiments are affection, enjoyment, and warmth towards others. Happiness is the script of continuing to do what we are doing, of what Barbara Fredrickson has called broadening our concerns and building our resources.[30] Most importantly, happiness is the emotion of cooperation. Its most intense sentiment is love, a script of being united with another person, and making that person's concerns one's own. Sadness is the emotion of reaction to loss of a loved other. Its script is of withdrawal, and gradual disconnection from aspects of life that had been shared. The emotions of lack of affection are coldness and disdain.

Interest and curiosity

Although in our very social species, most emotions are social scripts and commitments for certain kinds of relating, some emotions concern the physical world. Included are interest, curiosity, and what might be called the aesthetic emotions. Interest and curiosity are motivations of immense importance, the bases of our being able to engage in many kinds of plans, including those of our working life. Engagement in what interests us, and the pursuit of matters about which we are curious, can be sources of many kinds of positive emotions.[31] The aesthetic emotions are those that attract us to beauty.[32] Among the biases towards what we take to be beauty are those that attract us not just to faces of a certain kind,[33] but also to landscapes. As our ancestors started to walk upright, they moved out of the forests and onto open savannahs. Our human genes, it seems, still bias us towards preferences for savannah-like scenes. In an experiment, Orians and Heerwagen found that American children who were shown photographs of different landscapes preferred savannah to other types of landscape, although they had never seen a savannah personally.[34] It seems that such preferences are part of our genetic makeup, and they have been visible in landscape paintings since the Renaissance.[35]

Our ancestors came to prefer regions that promised food and water – flowers provide indications of fertile soil – and preferred also to be able to look out for predators or other potentially hostile hominid groups. We also like path-like features that hint at somewhere accessible that could be explored. Views with lookouts are thought of as prospects, and we like them still today, both in paintings, and if we have the opportunity to build a house.[36] Our ancestors also preferred shade and regions that offered refuge from threats. Here is the idea of the safe home base from which explorations can be made.

Contempt and hatred

Us and them: the root of much of the world's evil. The antidotes are I and thou, us and us. We human beings have inherited the proclivity to cooperate and to be kind to members our own group, and we must hope for evolutionary growth of this bias, as well as its cultivation in the societies in which we live. But in evolutionary terms, the corollary of this bias seems to have been a proclivity to deny the humanity of those outside our social group.[37] Perhaps the greatest challenge to our species is to become able to treat all people as people, in the same way that we would ourselves like to be treated.

Those emotions persisting from previous phases of our evolution that are directed antagonistically to those outside our community are the most dangerous in our repertoire. They are the emotions of contempt, hatred, and disgust. We inherit their legacy along with our capacity to love. Their most baleful expression is war, an activity that, in the twenty-first century, we still eagerly pursue. Maneuvering for status in the dominance hierarchy is a social act, with rules and procedures. By contrast, the emotions of contempt and hatred seek to eliminate the other, without constraint, as we would seek to obliterate a pest. Our promptings towards such acts are not social emotions. They are anti-social emotions.

It had been thought that we humans were the only mammals that killed members of our own species. It was a shock when Jane Goodall reported that such killings were also within the repertoire of the chimpanzees at Gombe.[38] A gang (one need use no other term) of chimpanzees patrolled the group's territory, and was observed to set upon and kill other chimpanzees in inferior numbers from a neighboring social group whom they encountered. One can argue that the emotion of hatred did once have a use, perhaps when factions within a band of hunter-gatherers fell out with each other, and emotions of this kind drove the two groups towards separate territories. Perhaps this was a spur to dispersal. Perhaps hatred had genetic consequences when our ancestors confronted other related hominid species such as the Neanderthals, who occupied the same areas of Europe as anatomically modern humans before becoming extinct about 30,000 years ago, along with all the other hominids, excepting our direct ancestors. There are two theories to account for this extinction. One is of interbreeding between our human ancestors and Neanderthals. The other is genocide: Neanderthals were killed off by ancestral humans motivated by the emotion of murderous contempt, equipped with language, with better weapons, and more cunning.

In terms of numbers and the extent of suffering, perhaps the most fateful and destructive clash that we know of in historical time was that between Europeans and Native Americans. Before Christopher Columbus landed in the Caribbean, in 1492, advance guard of large European invasions, it is estimated that the native population of the Americas was about 100 million. A century later, as Ronald Wright describes, it was about 10 million.[39] To sense the scale of this, imagine half the people you know in your generation dying. Some of this genocide took place by killing in scenes of extraordinary cruelty, by superior weapons-technology of the warlike invaders, who thought the natives were heathens who had no right to exist. Some accounts have been preserved from those times of the Spanish cutting down unarmed people with their swords. The combination of armed men facing others who have inferior weaponry or are in inferior numbers who are different to them is an invitation to draw from the human evolutionary well of murderous cruelty.

The majority of Native Americans died, however, not from force of arms, but from European infectious diseases to which they had no immunity. Even this was exploited by Europeans, who invented germ warfare by deliberately distributing to native people sheets that had been infected with smallpox.[40]

The European conquest of the Americas should also be read about in Jared Diamond's book *Guns, germs, and steel,*[41] in which the author asks the question: why did Europeans invade America, rather than Americans invade Europe and the Middle East? The answer is that the same people who invented the first writing, the Sumerians, were members of the groups who first domesticated plants and animals for food. They built the first cities, and they invented the first efficient metallurgy that led to steel swords. The successors of the Sumerians were the technologically sophisticated civilizations of Europe, who, by the time of the Renaissance, were able to take raiding parties across the Atlantic. For the Native Americans, domestication of food, city building, and metallurgy occurred thousands of years too late for them to do the same.

If Aztecs had invaded Europe and the Middle East in, say, 3000 BC, with a superiority of literacy and weaponry, and a cargo of deadly germs, there is no reason to think that the fate of this combined region would have been different from the fate of the Americas. A few impressive buildings would have survived – the Pyramids, Babylonian and Minoan palaces, Stonehenge – and some remnants of writing. But the ancient ways would have been replaced by a dwindling indigenous population, an alien religion, and an occupier's administration.

In the mid-1990s, Claude Lévi-Strauss, one of the most famous anthropologists of the twentieth century, wrote a retrospective article that he accompanied by photographs of the Nambikwara people of central Brazil, whom he visited in the 1930s. He writes: "Those about to browse through these photographs must be warned against [an] illusion: the belief that the Indians whom I show completely naked ... give us an accurate vision of primitive humanity."[42] In fact, far from being primitive, as early as the sixteenth century these people had a flourishing urban civilization. In 1541 a group of 50 Spaniards in search of food had let themselves be carried by the current down the river we now know as the Amazon. The chronicler, Friar Gaspar de Carvajal, records that for 3,000 kilometers, on either side of the river, "veritable cities appeared before their eyes...each city spread over several leagues along the banks of the river and comprised hundreds of houses of dazzling whiteness "[43] Subsequent accounts corroborate these observations, but they were forgotten. Thus was the contempt of the invaders matched by the contempt of subsequent European colonizers. When the wave of anthropological explorers arrived in the twentieth century, what they really saw, said Lévi-Strauss, were

> ...not examples of archaic ways of life that have been miraculously preserved for millennia, but the last escapees from the cataclysm that discovery and subsequent invasions had been for their ancestors. Imagine, keeping everything in proportion, scattered groups of survivors after an atomic holocaust on a planetary scale, or collision with a meteorite such as the one that, they say, caused the extinction of the dinosaurs.[44]

Mixtures of Motivations

When social motivations – assertion, attachment, affiliation – are exhibited on their own, we tend to regard them as pathological. A person who is only assertively powerful is intolerable, a fascist. A person who values only the safety of attachment is clingy, and is in the extreme an agoraphobic whose anxiety keeps the attachment partner close at hand. A person who is only affiliative can be seen as charming but feckless.

Motivations combine easily. A good mother is assertive, protective, and affiliative, and can be all three of these simultaneously. A good boss has status and power, but is also affiliatively concerned for those who work for him. An athlete may be extremely aggressive and also affiliative with team-mates. An artist has an intense interest in his or her medium, plus both competitive and affiliative relations to others. Mixtures of social and antisocial motivations also occur: assertive aggression plus contempt is especially important. They may offer raw materials for warrior castes, or volatile mixtures in civil society.

In addition, emotions that derive from the different kinds of motivation succeed each other, and when they do, they follow narrative sequences: so, for instance, in a typical action story, the pain and shame of some harm is succeeded by anger, then revenge, then some relief, and typically either reintegration or loneliness.

Ordinarily we move in a space of several motivations. Let me here just illustrate one kind of mixture, that of assertion and affiliation. The actions of the charging chimpanzee Yeroen described in the section of assertion make it seem as if being the alpha male is a matter merely of power. But this is not so. Yeroen had been the alpha male in the group for more than two years when, in 1976, something began to change. Yeroen had previously received between 75 and 90 percent of all submissive greetings in the group. He had the loyalty of all nine of the group's adult females. Then, in the spring of that year, the second male in the group (the beta male), Luit, stopped making submissive greetings to Yeroen. What happened over the next three months was that Luit gradually began to win over the females by a mixture of affection, bullying, and defiance of Yeroen. A third and younger male, Nikkie, also began to side with Luit. In the end Yeroen had no support, and Luit became the alpha.

Only twice during the period of the take-over were there physical fights between Luit and Yeroen. On both occasions they occurred while they were in their sleeping quarters, which Yeroen and Luit shared. On these occasions Yeroen emerged in the morning with wounds. Though they were not serious, he looked pitiful. He had lost his confidence. On the morning when the wounds were seen, Luit reacted with fear, went to visit each of the females in turn, then spent a large part of the day tending to Yeroen's injuries. Chimpanzees are assertive, and they can be aggressive, but for the most part, as soon as a rift has occurred, each is desperate to reconcile (see the opening illustration). In monkeys chemical manipulations that promote serotonin (as discussed in the previous chapter) have been found to enable lower ranking males to become the alpha animals in their groups.[45] This occurs by an increase of social confidence which includes aggression, but with concurrent promotion of affiliative activity such as grooming, to form alliances that are necessary for the alpha position.

We humans resist being moved downwards in status. When it happens we signal it, by shame and or embarrassment, which are distinguishable but involve some of the same gestures of deference that may be seen in our primate cousins. As Dacher Keltner and his collaborators have shown, displays of shame and embarrassment are distinct. They function to signal that one knows one has committed a social transgression, and willingness to appease and or to repair what had gone wrong. Socially, this is likely to bring about forgiveness and reconciliation, and the reinforcement of the mores of the social group.[46]

Compassion

Among our most quintessentially social kinds of emotion are not specific emotions, but the ability to feel what another feels or might feel: sympathy, empathy, compassion. Rachel Sternberg has explored the ways in which pity and compassion occurred in public life in ancient times, for instance in speeches in law courts, in attitudes to the sick, and to the defeated in war.[47] The following, for example, is from the fourth-century BC Athenian patriot Demosthenes, who observed people of his own side in a fierce war:

> It's a terrible, miserable sight, men of Athens. When we were travelling to Delphi recently, we couldn't avoid seeing it all – houses demolished, town walls removed, a country deprived of men of military age, a few poor women and children and pitiful old people; in short nobody could find words to describe the distress that there is in that country now.[48]

Here, history has not changed. One imagines again, from 500 years ago, the cities of Native Americans along the Amazon. One imagines today traveling to Kabul or Baghdad.

The fact that nowadays, we are utterly repelled by such scenes, seems to indicate an important cultural progress in the history of human emotions: a progress perhaps of empathy, in which we emotionally to understand what it is to be the other. David Konstan has argued that pity (nowadays we would say compassion) has changed since ancient times. In those times one could feel pity for people on one's own side in a war, as did Demosthenes, but not on the other,[49] and slavery was thought of not only as necessary but also as natural. Progress was not rapid: slaves in the American South were emancipated less than 150 years ago. In these and other reforms of the nineteenth century, empathy and compassion, as prompted by novelists and reformers, worked to change some of society's long-entrenched institutions.

We get a glimpse of ancient empathy in *The Iliad*, that tale of war between Europeans (Greeks) and a different society (Trojans, Asians in what is now Turkey). Towards the end of the story, the aggressive Achilles allows King Priam to come and retrieve the body of his son Hector, whom Achilles has slain. We see it too in the Indian epic *The Mahabarata*, when the victors who have thought themselves as representing the good in the noble fight against evil experience remorse as they realize that in their bloodthirstiness they too have become evil.[50] Both of these glimpses occurred only after the destruction has been wrought. Cruelty, as we see it the Nazi Holocaust and the ethnic cleansing of the former Yugoslavia, is still in modern times tall, strong, and vigorous. What has changed is that, although still an immature child, Empathy can now stand alongside Cruelty.

In the Greco-Roman tradition we humans define ourselves as beings who think: so the word "man" derives from *mens*, meaning mind. Arab tradition gets closer to the center, I think. In Arabic, the root name of a human being derives from the word for sympathy.[51] In terms of the history of this idea, the medieval Arabs in southern Spain were among the first to form societies in which there was tolerance among Muslims, Jews, and Christians.[52]

Adam Smith, discussed the emotions of sympathy and empathy in his book *The theory of moral sentiments*,[53] and thought they were the glue that holds society together. We are able to experience these emotions precisely because our emotions of love, of anger, of sadness, of fear, are universal, based on inherited systems of the limbic system; we share them with each other. We do not need to look far inside ourselves to see, and even experience, what another may be feeling. A strong argument can be made that morality is based on such empathetic emotions.[54] Children as young as 1 will offer comfort to another child. Although the youngest children tend to offer comfort in the way that they themselves like to be comforted, by the age of 3, they begin to recognize the individuality of the other, for instance by fetching a parent of the child who is crying. In one set of observations in day care, children were observed to comfort other children who cried. This was not true, however, for children who had a history of being abused. When these children saw someone else crying, then would often hit the crying child.[55] Thus does our individual history affect our capacities for caring about others.

CHAPTER SIX

Individual Histories

Emotional Development from Childhood to Maturity

John Keats, reading at his house, Wentworth Place, in Hampstead.
Source: *Posthumous portrait of John Keats (1823) by Joseph Severn.*

Origins of Identity

The common cognomen of this world among the misguided and superstitious is "a vale of tears" from which we are to be redeemed by a certain arbit[r]ary interposition of God and taken to heaven – What a little circumscribe[d] straightened notion! Call the world if you Please "The Vale of Soul Making". Then you will find out the use of this world.... How then are Souls to be made? How then are these sparks which are God to have identity given them – so as ever to possess a bliss peculiar to each ones individual existence? How but by the medium of a world like this?[1]

So wrote John Keats on April 21, 1819 from the house in which he lived in Hampstead on the edge of London, to his brother George and sister-in-law Georgiana, who had recently emigrated to the United States. A few weeks after writing this passage Keats would write some of his best known poems, including the "Ode to a Nightingale" and "Ode to a Grecian Urn."

In his letter, Keats refers to "sparks." He draws on the 2,000-year-old idea that the center of each of us is a spark, a little piece of God that has been detached and enclosed in a human body. According to a number of religious traditions, including the Christian one, our task on earth is to realize this, and make our journey upwards again to reunite our small spark with the great Divine.

Nowadays we might say that we each start with a random shake of the genetic dice, and find ourselves with this or that body in this or that time and place. So how do we attain an identity, what Keats calls a Soul? By taking responsibility for who we are despite the fact that we have had nothing to do with how we were produced, and with that responsibility to take part in "a world like this."

The idea of the spark of the divine, of which Keats wrote, emerged from a fusion of ideas from Babylon, Persia, Egypt, and from Jewish sources in Hellenistic culture around the time of the founding of Christianity. These religious ideas are known collectively as "Gnostic," where the term means knowledge of the divine within us.[2] Rather than the idea of the divine as rationality, which the Stoics believed, the Gnostic idea was more radical. It contained the notion of redemption by recognition of our divine origins. It reflected an aspiration among ordinary people to recognize their own worth, not just to be pawns in hierarchical societies. Christianity is one of the products of this movement. One of the most beautiful expressions of the idea of the divine spark is a poem by Andrew Marvell which puts the idea of the soul as a drop of dew that has condensed from the heavens onto a rose, and then, with the rising of the sun, is inhaled again into the sky. The turning point of the poem comes at the end of the development of the idea of the drop of dew, and proposes that the human soul has the same properties:

> And so the Soul, that Drop, that Ray
> Of the clear Fountain of Eternal Day,
> Could it within the humane flow'r be seen,
> Remembering still its former height
> Shuns the sweet leaves and blossoms green...[3]

One might regard all such talk as dualistic: that is to say, based on a regrettable separation of mind and body, which seems have derived in the first place from ancient Persia and which, despite modern research on the brain, continues to perplex us.[4] But if we regard such ideas as suggestive imagery that enables us to contemplate our predicament, we need not be scathing. One idea of what we moderns would call individual development and biography might be that each of us might wonder about shunning certain blandishments and "sweet leaves" of the physical world – first movements of emotions, sins – and make our way spiritually to reunite with a universal divine. The idea is well put by George Lord in his introduction to Marvell's poems. He says that Marvell expressed "on the one hand a passionate aspiration after something transient or unobtainable; on the other a cool and open-eyed recognition of the limitations of man's lot."[5] Though Lord applies this to Marvell, it has a more general significance. We each of us contend with twin aspects – call them if you like aspiration and actuality – in our journey through what Keats called "The Vale of Soul Making." If we are thoroughly post-Darwinian, we can cast the idea into terms used by Stanovich: how in our lives do we choose among actions that represent who we are as people, versus those forces that are purely the product of the replicators that are our genes?

Four Components of Character

What influences can be identified in the history of character formation in a post-Darwinian world? In the following sections I consider four such influences on which there has been substantial research.

Chemical influences

It is a very ancient idea that temperament and character are determined by elements within us called humors which, in a relationship of microcosm (each individual) to macrocosm (the universe), imitate the elements of the outer world. The elements were: blood, which corresponds to air; yellow bile, which corresponds to fire; black bile, which corresponds to earth; and phlegm, which corresponds to water. Character was determined by the balance among these four.[6] With severe imbalances, illness occurs, and then one or more of the elements – blood, bile, or phlegm – could become frankly visible. The notion of four character traits based on the same four ancient humors continues today in English, respectively as sanguine (hopeful and confident), choleric (irascible), melancholic (depressive), and phlegmatic (even-tempered). The idea of humors is very much alive in neuroscience, in which we think in terms of hormones, peptides, and transmitter substances (discussed in Chapter 4). The influence of substantial amounts of serotonin in our system, for instance, which to some extent we inherit as a genetic bias, produces a character who is sanguine: hopeful and socially confident.

Variation was an essential component of Darwin's mechanism of evolution, and it is accomplished by genetic mixing. In the production of each new human being the genes of one parent are mixed more or less randomly with those of the other parent. Except for identical twins (known technically as monozygotic twins, because they derive from the same zygote: the fusion of egg and sperm), we are all genetically different. Even identical twins, though their similarities with each other are substantial, become uniquely themselves because their experiences differ.

Temperament is the emotional style we come in with. So, as parents know, one infant is irritable and affected by any deviation from routines (perhaps one might say choleric) while another is easy-going and placid (phlegmatic). Temperament is genetically given. It has been measured in a number of ways. One set of traits is offered by Hill Goldsmith. The traits are emotional: Social Fearfulness (shyness), Anger Proneness, Pleasure (based on positive emotions including smiling and laughing), and Interest/Persistence (which is also thought of in terms of emotion regulation). It was found that monozygotic twins were likely to be similar on each of these scales and, except for Pleasure, substantially more likely to be similar than twins who came from different fertilized eggs (dizygotic twins).[7] What this means is that for the traits other than Pleasure, the major influence is genetic rather, than, for instance, the emotional influence of the family. If the environment of the family were the predominant influence, dizygotic twin infants of the same sex would be expected to be almost as similar in temperament as monozygotic twins. The positive emotions in the infant and toddler (Pleasure) do indeed seem to derive from family environment as much as, or more than, from genes. The likely influence in this case is the personality of the mother.

The most important empirical work to explore the idea of a persistence of certain kinds of temperament was done by Avshalom Caspi and colleagues, who followed up two groups of people who were assessed as children at age 8, and again 30 years later.[8] One set was very shy in childhood. The males in this group continued to be shy as adults: they were on average slower to get jobs or to marry, or to become fathers, than non-shy men. Women who were shy also continued shy as adults, but they did not do worse than their non-shy age-mates. They spent less time in the workforce than average. They tended to marry men who had higher career status, perhaps because they were prepared to fulfill traditional roles of wife and mother.

More striking were the children who were angry at age 8, and who had frequent temper outbursts. Thirty years later they tended still to be ill-tempered. On average, compared with non-angry people, they were less likely to stay in school and had more erratic work lives, leading to downward social mobility and lower occupational status. Ill-tempered women also did relatively more badly than non-angry age-mates. They married below their social class expectations, had less marital satisfaction, and were more ill-tempered as parents than those who were non-angry at age 8.

In a recent study that linked facial expressions to stability of personality, Harker and Keltner assessed the happiness of expressions in pictures in a women's college yearbook.[9] Positive emotional expressions in the yearbook photos predicted well-being at age 21, 27, 43, and 52. Women who expressed positive emotions in their yearbook photo experienced fewer psychological and physical difficulties during their young and middle adulthood, had better relations with others, and generally felt more satisfied with their lives. Notice that a positive expression is not just an outward and visible expression of an inward emotional state. It is an invitation to take part in a cooperative relationship.

It is perhaps regrettable – though what can one say? – that the number of distinct traits of personality generally recognized in modern research in adults is no longer four. This was the number preferred by the ancient Pythagoreans and theorists of humors. Now the number of separable traits of personality is thought to be five, and a great deal of research has gone into establishing this. The idea of personality is essentially the same as that of temperament, but extended into adult life. The idea is that there are traits of personality that persist across time, that are displayed in different circumstances, that are influenced by genetics and the chemicals via which that influence is transmitted. The five traits each have an emotional core. They are: Neuroticism (proneness to anxiety, hostility, and depression), Extroversion (warmth, sociability, cheerfulness), Openness (to fantasies, emotions, aesthetics, ideas), Agreeableness (responsiveness to others including trust and compliance), and Conscienciousness (including striving for achievement, dutifulness, self discipline). The authors of the five-factor personality scheme, Costa and McCrae, present evidence that everyday mood is related to people's personality as measured on these traits.[10] They put the following question: "How will you feel two months and three days after your 78th birthday?" They say that people tend to say either that they will feel old, or that it would depend on circumstances such as their health. Costa and McCrae say that both answers are wrong: they are likely to feel much as they feel today, because both personality and mood have a continuity with the temperament that could have been observed in childhood.

Well and good; but to understand a life, our own or someone else's, this does not seem to be all. We want to ponder the issue put by Keats. We would like to know how, with the throw of the genetic dice that affects our temperament, might experience of "a world like this" touch us, and enable us to become who we are: kind to others, shy, or aggressive. Each human being is unique not just in having a face that is recognizable or in having a prevailing mood, but in being touched by a unique set of emotional experiences and expressing responses to these experiences in a way that can be seen as individual.

Attachment and emotional templates

Attachment theory was introduced in the previous chapter. It was Bowlby's idea that part of the inheritance of humans is a system that enables a close emotional bonding in infancy with a caregiver, typically a mother. In this theory, Bowlby was concerned with the idea that early emotional development lays foundations for adult emotional relationships. The deprivation of a continuous, warm, and loving relationship with a mother or other caregiver does indeed put a person at considerable risk for a life of psychiatric and other problems.

In part this idea derives from Freud: each early relationship of any importance forms, as it were, an emotional template from which later relationships, later attitudes, later fears and hopes, will be patterned. Freud's first substantial exposition of the idea came in his first full-length case history, that of Dora.[11] She was a young woman who was sent to see Freud by her father in the Fall of 1900, because she was suffering from what we would now call an eating disorder, and because her parents had found a suicide note. It was in this case that Freud constructed his theory of transference, which became the core principle of psychoanalytic therapy. His idea for therapy was that the patient will tend to interact with the therapist by means of the same emotions that formed the relationship with a parent, but that these movements of relating are unconscious. Thus Dora began by wanting to be intimate with Freud, but then found him untrustworthy. She decided he had let her down, and she rejected him. This was exactly the pattern that she had formed with her father, and that she repeated with a family friend, Herr K, who had paid court to her. Therapy consists in the analyst offering interpretations, which are suggestions as to what the patient is unconsciously doing in the relationship. The biographical version of this idea is that such template-influenced patterns of relating occur not just in therapy but in many, if not all, adult relationships.

Bowlby was working as a psychoanalyst at the Tavistock Clinic in London when he developed the beginnings of attachment theory, and he placed an advertisement in *The Times* for a research assistant. The person offered the job was Mary Ainsworth, who immersed herself in the idea of attachment and made important contributions to it. After her work with Bowlby, and after she had returned to USA, she furthered the idea of early relationships as templates by describing distinct styles of attachment in 1-year-old infants who were exposed to what is known as "the strange situation."[12] The strange situation is in fact a laboratory room. At first the infant enters the room with his or her mother. Then a researcher, a stranger, enters and sits quietly. A few minutes later the mother leaves. The stranger then tries to interact with the infant. A few minutes after this, the mother returns and the researcher leaves. In the next phase the mother leaves, and says "Bye-bye." Then the researcher returns and tries again to interact with the infant. Ainsworth and her collaborators recognized three styles of emotionality of infants in the strange situation. One they called secure. An infant with this style was distressed at separation from her or his mother, but when the mother returned the baby sought her and could be comforted by her. The researchers called a second style ambivalently attached. When the mother of such an infant returned after the separation, the infant wanted to be with her but was angry, and refused to be comforted. A third style was called avoidantly attached. An infant with this style made no attempt to interact with the mother when she returned.

Later a fourth attachment style was added: the disorganized style, which may in reality be not so much a style of attachment as a category for children whose early life had been chaotic. These were children who had not formed a reliable attachment relationship with a caregiver, or who had been subjected to neglect and/or abuse.

Ainsworth's idea of attachment styles is, therefore, an empirical version of Freud's template idea. In a study by Waters et al. testing this critically,[13] by seeing whether people had styles of relating as adults that are similar to those of their infancy, 60 white middle-class people who had been classified in the strange situation as infants were given an adult attachment interview at the age of 21. This interview was designed to assess their experience of intimate relationships in adulthood. Seventy-two percent of the people in the study maintained their style of secure versus insecure attachment.

Scripts

The idea of scripts is taken from the theater, from the idea of a set of lines from which a role can be enacted. It has been important in psychology at least since 1977, when Roger Schank and Robert Abelson discussed it.[14] We can think of a script as a narrative-like sequence that affords an understanding of familiar kinds of episodes in which a protagonist enacts plans based on goals, and experiences their outcomes. A script, then, is a sequence that tends to be performed over and over again. Waking up, going to the bathroom, putting on clothes, having breakfast – in whatever way and whatever order one habitually does these – is a script. In previous chapters, I used the idea of script to describe the outline, or frame, for interpersonal relations that is set up by an emotion: happiness sets up a script for cooperation, anger sets up conflict, and so on.

Sylvan Tomkins developed the idea of emotion-based life scripts.[15] His approach has three parts. First, he thought that emotions are the real motivators of behavior. We have many different motivations, but it is only when an emotion takes a hold of one of them and amplifies it that our behavior becomes fully directed. Second, when an emotion is in progress it recruits a whole set of processes in the brain and body to orchestrate the response, which occurs as a package. So, in a sexual response, the face is alive, the mind engaged, the sexual organs are excited. In most emotions, Tomkins thought the face was a special marker: expressing happiness, anger, fear, sadness, and so on. Third, Tomkins argued that people act according to scripts to solve certain kinds of emotional problems in their lives. Once a person is lodged in a particular script, it becomes a core component of the personality, in which a sequence can be triggered by any one element.

One example is what Tomkins calls the sedation script. When there is a negative emotion, the person moves to dampen it down, sedate it. For different people this script might be performed by having a cigarette, by alcohol, by turning on the television. There are also many other kinds of scripts: a person with a power script is one who reacts to negative emotions by becoming angry; a person with a script of helping others might feel empathetic with their negative emotions and try to solve their problems.

Sedation scripts have the purpose of escaping from a negative emotion, be it boredom, loneliness, anxiety, sadness. They can develop into what Tomkins calls pre-addictive scripts. In these, the sedation response is used not just to escape but also to avoid. So a person might avoid the anxiety of social interaction by becoming a compulsive television watcher, avoid anxieties about whether he or she is loved by seeking frequent sexual encounters, and so forth. In a full-blown addictive script, the activity that was sedating or avoiding becomes important for its own sake. A person becomes a drunk, a career gambler, a compulsive seeker of sexual encounters.

A script combines features of habit with that of a narrative episode. Habit, as William James pointed out, is one of the most important of psychological processes. Like the creases on a jacket or pair of shoes, its shape persists once it is formed.[16] It becomes both a comfort and a constraint.

Script-habits gather around emotions or, to put it the other way round, we each, in our early years, form the beginning of our personality around a temperament and emotional style, which typically includes the style of our attachment relationship and other elements of family upbringing.

Jennifer Jenkins has proposed that for each person a predominating emotion script (or emotion schema) can develop as a balance among different systems of social emotional goals.[17] For instance, children who grow up in families in which aggressive coercion is the norm,[18] or in which there has been much angry conflict between their parents, form what she calls an anger organization: one that is dominated by anger as compared with other social emotions such as attachment or affection. Children with an anger organization tend predominantly to evaluate events as frustrations, slights, and insults. They are prone, then, to retaliate, and to be aggressive.[19] Both mothers and teachers report such children to show a lot of anger and aggression and, by contrast, low levels of sadness or anxiety.

These are children who, as Caspi and his colleagues (discussed above) showed, had a high probability of carrying forward their aggression into adult life.

Dynamic systems

A new kind of theory in child development is dynamic systems theory, which is related to chaos theory, a topic of recent scientific interest. It includes the idea that certain systems organize themselves and maintain continuity through time, even though events impinging on them are unpredictable. Weather systems are well thought of in these terms. The use to which dynamic systems theory is put in understanding a person's emotional individuality includes three ideas that have been described by Marc Lewis and his colleagues.[20]

First is the idea of an attractor. Imagine a ball rolling in a bowl-shaped region. However you start it off, the ball rolls towards the lowest place, which is called an attractor. Once the ball is in one attractor region it tends to stay there. The idea is comparable to that of a script or schema, described above. The ball needs a strong push to get it into another region, say an adjacent valley, a movement that can be called a phase shift. A cheerful person who has occasions of sadness would have both a happy and a sad attractor region, and a question might be how to move to the happy region when one had become sad. One may imagine also surfaces that include hills, which are repellor regions. A person who tends to be angry can be thought of as having an angry attractor region, comparable to Jenkins's idea of an anger organization. If this person also had great sensitivity to shame, he or she might have a repellor hill of shame avoidance growing out of the region.

Next, the development of an individual history can be thought of in terms of pathways that branch. One might start off on a path in an optimistic direction but some adversity might press one to take a fork towards a region of anxiety. Then, consciously or unconsciously, decisions might be made to take further forks in the path that avoid anything that might seem dangerous or threatening: stay home rather than go out, take the safe alternative, don't risk anything unknown. The path of caution, on one side of the set of possibilities, then would diverge further and further from paths that involved risks and assertiveness. One group of the 8-year-olds studied by Caspi and his colleagues took paths of social caution and shyness, while the other group took paths of anger. By the time they reached adulthood, neither could easily reach paths other than those they were on.

A third idea from the world of complexity theory is that of fractals. A pattern at one scale occurs also at other scales. Thus a branching pattern can be seen through a microscope as you look at the veins on a leaf. You can see a similar pattern as you look from a hundred yards away at an oak tree in winter. In another example, the irregular pattern of rocks and sand that forms the border of a seashore is reproduced again at a different scale if you look at a map. So it is in personality. On a small scale, a certain stance, an assertive gesture and facial expression, can occur at the larger scale in a person's life of getting one's own way by bullying and competitiveness.

Emotions as the Bases of Personality

One of the most interesting works of recent psychology is Carol Magai and Jeannette Haviland-Jones's book *The hidden genius of emotion*.[21] In it the authors do no less than rewrite the psychological bases of personality and its transformations. They take the lives of three men, each the inventor of an influential school of psychotherapy. One is Carl Rogers, founder of client-centered therapy and of the counseling approach to psychotherapy. The second is Albert Ellis, founder of rational-emotive therapy, one of the tributaries of cognitive behavioral therapy (discussed in Chapter 3), which is now accepted as the most effective kind of psychotherapy for emotional disorders. The third is Fritz Perls, founder of Gestalt therapy, a lively version of psychoanalysis from which has derived emotion-focused psychotherapy.

Magai and Haviland-Jones took the materials of attachment theory, script theory, and dynamic systems theory to write emotion-based biographies of these three men. Each man had written autobiographically, and for each other material was available about their lives and relationships. As well as discovering emotional themes in biographical events, Magai and Haviland-Jones analyzed for emotional themes these men's autobiographical writings and also three scholarly books, one each from early, middle, and late in each one's career.

Serendipitously, the three men appeared in the earliest movie made to show what goes on in psychotherapy.[22] The film has three parts. In each, one of the therapists spoke to the camera to introduce his form of psychotherapy, worked for a half-hour session with a client, Gloria, who had recently separated from her husband, and then spoke to the camera to say something about how he thought the session had gone. Among the striking attributes of this film is the way in which the personalities of the three men fairly leap off the screen. Rogers listens respectfully to Gloria. Ellis lectures at her. Perls berates her. For Magai and Haviland-Jones, the film was a gift that allowed them to use the most researched of all aspects of emotions, the analysis of facial expressions,[23] to contribute to the theory of how emotions and emotionality form the bases of personality.

Carl Rogers

Let me here offer some of Magai and Haviland-Jones's analyses of one of the people they chose: Carl Rogers. He was born in Oak Park, Illinois, in 1902, into a well-off fundamentalist Christian family. He was the fourth of six children, and the baby of the family for five years. He was so sickly as a child that his parents worried that he might not survive. At the age of 22 he graduated from university and two months later began a long, and for the most part happy, marriage with a woman he had known in adolescence. He went on to an extraordinarily successful professional career. He developed a new kind of therapy that departed radically from other approaches of the time, based on listening with understanding and empathy to a person without the psychoanalytic objective of making interpretations of what was going on in the unconscious. His method became the basis of counseling psychology. He was the first person to do empirical research in psychotherapy, by tape recording sessions. He also was a leader in the encounter group movement.

In his autobiography he wrote: "As a person I see myself as fundamentally positive in my approach to life; somewhat of a lone wolf in my professional activities, socially rather shy, but enjoying close relationships."[24] His wife wrote that as a teenager he had been "shy, sensitive, and unsocial."[25] Many people found him a gentle person, remarkably devoid of anger. At the same time some professional colleagues found him "an irritant of monumental proportions."[26] During his academic career he moved to new positions several times, probably to escape interpersonal conflicts that had arisen in professional relationships.

These are the conventional materials of biography: facts of birth order, family, marriage, and career, ideas culled from autobiography, reminiscences of those who knew the person. What binds such materials together, and allows us to understand them? For Magai and Haviland-Jones, the binding is supplied by continuities of attachment, script theory, and emotional attractor regions:

> ... it appears that Rogers's primary attachment relationship was secure, versus avoidant or ambivalent. Yet, his interactions with other social partners could be fractious. ... Rogers could also be painfully shy, and yet he was drawn to people and even did group encounter therapies. He often made others the center of his existence. He was also often in conflict with others, but he was not a particularly "angry" or hostile man.[27]

Magai and Haviland-Jones see Rogers as developing a script in which there was a longing for close relationships, but also a great deal of shame. They infer that the shame derived from his fundamentalist Christian upbringing, in which it would be induced frequently by a mother who was always ready to recognize shortcomings. The family in which Rogers grew up was one in which emotions were not valued, and anger not tolerated. Rogers's intimate attachment script was augmented, one might say, by what Tomkins has called disillusionment. Having been enclosed in the paradise of a warm and protective relationship when he was an infant, this atmosphere was lost when he reached the age of 6 or 7. At this point, he not only had to go to school but was now subject to teasing and competition by siblings. By no means amounting to a severe life event, such a disillusion might nevertheless prompt a person to take one path rather than another in life.

Rogers's emotional organization, then, can be thought of in terms of a large attractor area of interpersonal warmth and interest, with areas of shame repellors within it, and a very large mountain growing out of it (derived from family culture) by which anger is avoided.

Although many of us may have suspected that psychologists tend to specialize in topics in which they have some personal involvement, it has taken Magai and Haviland-Jones to show that for all three men whom they studied

> ...their own historical attachment patterns are reproduced in the context of the style of psychotherapy that they conduct. That is, Rogers creates a climate for secure relatedness. By contrast, Ellis [whom they infer had an anxiously avoidant attachment style] recreates a climate for detachment to emerge, and Perls [whose early life was chaotic] creates a climate for the turbulence of disorganized attachment leading to rapid change and potential phase shifts.[28]

Both Magai and Haviland-Jones had done a good deal of research on analyzing facial expressions. The film with Gloria allowed them to put their expertise to work. In his interview with Gloria, we see Rogers as we might expect: attentive, warm, supportive. His dominant facial expression is that of interest, but with eyebrows slightly slanted upwards towards the middle of his brow, to suggest sadness. If emotions offer scripts for relationships, his emotion is an invitation to take part in a relationship that includes talk of intimate matters. Gloria accepts the invitation. In doing so, she escapes the shame of self-criticism, and this is what Rogers offers: an opportunity for the client to move towards greater self-acceptance. Towards the end of the session Gloria told him that she felt she was able to talk to him in the way that she would like to have talked to her father, though that had never been possible for her. Rogers replied that to him she seemed like a pretty nice daughter.

Later Gloria said about the session:

> I felt my, uh, more lovable, soft, caring self with Dr Rogers. And, uh, I even felt more free openly, even about sex, and I was surprised by that.[29]

When Rogers summed up the session afterwards, he said he felt pleased by how it had gone. Magai and Haviland-Jones draw attention to a particular moment, when Rogers talked about how successful he had been. He said: "When I'm able to enter into a relationship, and I feel it was true in this instance..." His voice rose with the last few words, and Magai and Haviland-Jones comment:

> He was being spontaneous here and the excitement and proud pleasure mounted. At the height of this juncture, the configuration of his face changed into a more open and unguarded one, and at this point we see the only "pure" prototypic interest expression (brows raised and arched) of the whole film. Furthermore, what happened next is even more revealing. The raised brow lasted only a flicker of a second before the muscles controlling the outer brow were drawn into play to pull the outer corners down, thus creating the sad brow with the oblique configuration.[30]

A page beforehand they had proposed the fractal idea: a pattern of a fleeting facial expression can be repeated in the pattern of a life:

> A person's face is not just the locus of both fleeting and sustained emotional reactions but also an historical document, revealing lifelong patterns of emotional expression and inhibition...and the dynamic interplay between historical events and learning experiences.

Nearly a century before, Proust had put the same idea like this:

> The features of our face are hardly more than gestures which force of habit has made permanent. Nature, like the destruction of Pompeii, like the metamorphosis of a nymph, has arrested us in an accustomed movement.[31]

What this glimpse of Rogers's excitement inhibited by shame showed, in miniature, was an aspect of the dynamics of his emotional script-organization: it is shameful to express too much excitement or pride. Rogers shows far more shame than the other two therapists. His expressions include aversion of the eyes, and speech disfluencies (hesitations, ums and ers).

As well as his nurturing warmth and his shame, one has to consider Rogers's antagonisms with psychiatrists and other professional groups, in which he seemed to draw on a script of self-righteous exclusiveness that derived from his religious upbringing. He tended to treat outsiders with reserve and even contempt. Magai and Haviland-Jones ask how we might reconcile the various descriptions. "Was he warm or aloof? Caring or attacking? Social or shy? Mild or angry?"[32]

How does Magai and Haviland-Jones's idea compare with other approaches? Conventional theories of personality describe only the continuity of moods and behavioral tendencies, and are devoid of nuance. A psychoanalytically inclined biographer allows for more detail, but tends to search for, and then of course find, inner conflict. In Rogers, he or she might infer something like a repressed longing for power submerged beneath a mild social manner. I believe that these kinds of approach would not bring us much closer to who Carl Rogers was, or to an understanding of his work. By contrast, by basing their work on attachment styles, scripts, and dynamic systems theory, Magai and Haviland-Jones provide us with new insights, to show how emotions in interaction with "a world like this" can be the generative processes in the continuing development of personality.

Points of divergence

Once one has embarked on a certain life trajectory, why does one take this path rather than that one? There are several possibilities.

Among the most likely candidates are what are called life events: happenings that prompt changes in emotional tone, and divert one from a previous path. In Waters et al.'s study on the continuity of attachment style from infancy to adulthood mentioned above,[33] what seemed most closely associated with switching a child into a different attachment style was a negative life event such as loss of a parent, parental divorce, parental physical or psychiatric illness, and physical or sexual abuse. In a comparable study of the continuity of attachment of 57 people who were particularly at risk, and had high rates of negative life events – child maltreatment, depression in the mothers, and family malfunctioning in early adolescence – such events were found to be the major influence in changes from secure to insecure attachment styles between infancy and young adulthood.[34]

The "world like this" that John Keats experienced included plenty of such life events. At the age of 9, his father died. Six years later, after a long illness, so did his mother. At the age of 24, after he had nursed him through a long bout of tuberculosis, Keats's brother Tom died. Not long after this, at about the time he wrote the letter in which he meditated on the uses of "a world like this," he too became ill with the tuberculosis that would kill him just two years later.

Perhaps the most venerable means of choosing one path rather than another in life is reflection on one's life followed by the more-or-less deliberate decision to set off along some particular path. The reflection can be done alone, or accompanied by reading, or taken in conjunction with someone else, such as a therapist or teacher. Self-reflection was the process that prompted the Epicureans and Stoics not just to think about how people should live, but also to devote themselves to considered lives based on the principles they discovered.

Religious conversion experiences have typically been of this kind. They have summoned a person from a life of unthoughtfulness to a chosen path in life. Among the great historical personal documents of this kind is Augustine's *Confessions*.[35] A hundred years ago, William James in his *Varieties of religious experience*,[36] made a study of conversion experiences of the kind that Augustine underwent. James proposed the metaphor of the self as like a polyhedron (a solid with several flat faces). At any time in our lives it is as if we rest on one of the faces of the polyhedron (of complacency, of barely suppressed exasperation, of hedonistic self-indulgence). What happens in a religious conversion is that, sometimes with huge effort, the polyhedron is tipped over in the course of a powerful emotional experience and comes to rest on another face: perhaps of asceticism, perhaps of good works, perhaps of enlightenment. What James was talking about are the changes that dynamic systems theorists call phase shifts.

Towards the end of his book, James said: "In re-reading my manuscript, I am almost appalled at the amount of emotionality which I find in it." Using the metaphor "hot" to indicate a matter of strong emotional interest, he had written:

> Things hot and vital to us today are cold tomorrow. It is as if seen from the hot parts of the field that the other parts appear to us, and from these hot parts personal desire and volition make their sallies. They are in short the centres of our dynamic energy, whereas the cold parts leave us indifferent and passive in proportion to

their coldness. . . . Emotional occasions, especially violent ones, are extremely potent in precipitating mental rearrangements. The sudden and explosive ways in which love, jealousy, guilt, fear, remorse, or anger can seize upon one are known to everybody. Hope, happiness, security, resolve, emotions characteristic of conversion, can be equally explosive. And emotions that come in this explosive way seldom leave things as they found them.[37]

It was such emotions, James concluded, that can tip the polyhedron of self onto a different face, start a person along a new path. What philosophers such as Epicurus and Chrysippus taught was that such shifts could also be based on reason. Magai and Haviland-Jones argued that, towards the end of his life, Rogers was able to make a shift towards maintaining better terms with men who were not his patients. In this way, he was able resolve to some extent the inner contradiction between his nurturing self and his self-righteous and aloof self.

The most usual basis for taking one life path rather than another is a relationship, especially the relationship of falling in love. What love does, as a script, is to create a commitment that enlarges, as it were, the boundaries of the self to include the other, and to suspend or sometimes even to terminate commitments to people such as parents and previous lovers. Such a termination of her relationship with her father was wrought by Elizabeth Barrett when she fell in love with Robert Browning.

Among the most important empirical work on such matters is that of David Quinton and Michael Rutter, who followed up the lives of girls who had been brought up in institutions, and thereby had experienced disorganized early attachment without a stable attachment figure.[38] They compared these girls with others from the same social class background who had been brought up in normal families. As adults, 33 percent of those who grew up in institutions had handicapping psychiatric disorders, as compared with 5 percentof those who grew up in their own families. Being without a primary attachment person therefore puts one at considerable risk. When they became mothers themselves, the women who had been institutionalized as children tended to be insensitive to their own children, lacking in warmth, harsh and inconsistent. Similar transgenerational effects of lack of proper mothering have also been found in other mammals by Alison Fleming and her collaborators.[39]

Institutionalized girls had not, one might say, been inducted into the script during their own upbringing of a warm and reliable parent–child relationship, and had little idea of how to provide one for their children. There were exceptions, however: some women who had disorganized upbringings did function well as mothers. They were those who had formed a loving relationship in adulthood with men who could be supportive, in whom they could confide, and who could be relied upon to help.

Being without a loving relationship with at least one parent in early childhood does put one at risk, and tends to direct one on a certain kind of life path, of doing badly at school, of disorganized relationships and work life. Finding a loving relationship in adulthood can do much to repair the early damage. One is tempted to say that love, even at a later time in one's life, can enable one to take a path towards warmer and more reliable relationships, including relationships with one's children on which they themselves will depend.

CHAPTER SEVEN

Emotional Disorders

Excesses of Sadness, Anxiety, Shame, and Anger

Statue thought to be of Hippocrates, founder of the most famous Greek school of medicine, from the island of Cos, where he was born.

Depression

What we know of the history of emotional disorders in the West goes back 2,500 years, to Greek doctors in the school of Hippocrates. Here is a piece of one of their writings:

> A woman at Thasos became morose as the result of a justifiable grief, and although she did not take to her bed, she suffered from insomnia, loss of appetite, thirst and nausea. She lived on the level ground near Pylades' place. Early on the night of the first day, she complained of fears and talked much; she showed despondency, and a very slight fever. In the morning she had many convulsions; when the convulsions had for the most part ceased, she talked at random and used foul language.[1]

In classical Greece, many of the ways in which doctors now consider such episodes were already established. This account is from a case book. The genre in which the doctor wrote is that of a case history, or, in medical terms, simply a history, of how the patient became ill and what her symptoms were. "Symptom" means something of which a patient complains, or might complain. What we could call the emotional symptoms of this case were morose mood, insomnia, loss of appetite, fears. The physician includes something about where the woman lived – Thasos, on the level ground – and something about what caused the condition – a justifiable grief. A modern reader might think that the grief could have been due to a bereavement. A modern family doctor who saw someone with symptoms of morose mood, sleeplessness, lack of appetite, fears, would diagnose depression, prescribe sleeping pills and perhaps Prozac.

When the writer talks about "the first day," he means the first day of a fever – his principal interest – and the case history continues with a description of its course over the next few days. To a modern diagnostician it would seem likely that the patient had an infection, but it would not be clear from the ancient account whether this had anything to do with the initial depression. Therein lies a kind of problem that has been faced in understanding illnesses of many kinds. Which symptoms hang together to form a specific condition, and which have a different origin? The modern physician would again have something to prescribe: an antibiotic. If the infection were bacterial, there would be a good chance that the antibiotic would cure it within a day or two. It would, however, leave untouched the depression, which had started with a "justifiable grief."

When a depression was long-standing, the ancient Hippocratic doctors relied on the theory of humors that was already established in their time, and would refer to it as melancholia. Depression continued to be discussed in these terms during the Renaissance, for instance in the wide-ranging book by Shakespeare's contemporary Robert Burton, *The anatomy of melancholy*.[2] "Melancholy" has now been replaced by the term "major depression," which is sufficiently disabling that the sufferer cannot cope with ordinary living: cannot perform properly at work, or do ordinary tasks at home. Depression has a significant negative impact economically. The World Health Organization recently described it as the single most burdensome disease in the world, in terms of disability-adjusted life years among adults. In USA alone it has an estimated cost of $33 billion per year.[3]

One of the most important pieces of research on emotional disorders in the twentieth century, was published in the late 1970s by George Brown and Tirril Harris.[4] They found that major depression is caused by something going seriously wrong in a person's life: by what the Hippocratic physician attending the woman from Thasos called "justifiable grief."

Brown and Harris reported the results of a study of 458 women, randomly selected from voters' lists in South London, England. Women were chosen for this study because, in order to make the necessary analyses of the results, the researchers needed to have a substantial number of people who had become depressed, and the frequency of depression in women is nearly twice that of men. Researchers met with each woman to interview her and make a diagnosis. Here an example of one of the interviewees.

Mrs Trent had three small children and was married to a van driver. Her apartment had two rooms and a kitchen. A year before the interview she had occasional migraine headaches, but she felt quite herself. Her third child was born eight months before the interview. Around that time her husband lost his job. She didn't worry too much, and he got another job quickly. But after two weeks he was fired from that job too, without explanation. Mrs Trent thought it was because his previous firm had given him a bad reference that arrived only after he had started work. Seven weeks later her worries had become so severe that she felt tense all the time, miserable, unable to sleep, and irritable. She found it difficult to do the housework or look after the children. She became unable to concentrate, and her appetite declined. In the next two months these symptoms worsened. She would often cry during the day. She got some sleeping pills from her doctor. Her relationship with her husband deteriorated. She lost all interest in sex and thought her marriage finished. Three times she packed and walked out but returned because of the children. She felt self-deprecatory, felt she could not cope with anything, and thought that she might end it all.[5]

Mrs Trent was suffering from major depression. To diagnose a disorder, an interviewer asks the person in detail about a list of symptoms. The symptoms of depression mentioned in Mrs Trent's vignette, above, were: persistent sadness, tension, irritability, difficulty with sleeping, difficulty in concentration, loss of weight through loss of appetite, loss of interest in previously pleasurable activities, self-deprecation, and thoughts of suicide. A diagnosis of depression is made if, over a period of two weeks, a person is sad so that she or he bursts into tears a lot, and/or has lost all interest in things that were previously enjoyable, plus at least four other symptoms of the kind indicated above at levels that are disabling.[6] In ordinary terms Mrs Trent was in despair.

Of the 458 adult women interviewed by Brown and Harris's team, 8 percent had suffered a major depressive breakdown, with or without accompanying symptoms of anxiety, during the year before the interview. A further 9 percent had a major depressive disorder (depression or mixed depression and anxiety) that made them unable to cope and that had lasted more than a year.[7]

In a part of the interview different from that used to make the diagnosis, the women were asked about 40 areas of life – including employment, finances, housing, children, relationships – and whether adversities had occurred in each one. Adversities were divided into life events, sudden incidents like bereavements, and longer term difficulties such as having very little money. Each event and difficulty was written up as a brief vignette by the interviewer, who read it to the research team. This team rated the severity of the adversity in terms of how threatening it would be to the ordinary woman living in the circumstances of the interviewee. These adversities in adulthood are the equivalents of the life events of childhood and adolescence that were described in the previous chapter as capable of pushing a child off his or her developmental pathway.

What Brown and Harris found was that adverse events and difficulties that were judged to constitute a severe threat that lasted longer than a week were capable of provoking depression. Of the 37 women (from the 458 interviewed) who became depressed during the year before the interview, 33 had suffered such a severe event or difficulty. For Mrs Trent, for instance, the onset of depression was preceded by her husband's second job loss, which deprived the family of its income, with no prospect of any alternative means of livelihood.

When someone has a breakdown – often called a nervous breakdown[8] – it almost always involves depression, sometimes on its own, sometimes mixed with anxiety. It is not the daily hassles of life that cause breakdowns; it is adversity that is so severe as to deprive a person of the meaning of life. Studies subsequent to Brown and Harris's original one have discovered the kinds of adversities that are most potent in provoking both major depressions and anxiety disorders. They are:

- loss: events such as deaths of loved ones, losses of means of livelihood;
- humiliation: events such as separations in which there has been infidelity, or the delinquency of a child, rapes, put-downs and public humiliations by loved ones and persons in authority that threaten core roles;
- entrapment, in which a person is stuck in an adverse situation with no way out;
- danger, the likelihood of future loss, or of an event that has yet to realize its full potential.[9]

In terms of emotions, then, events and difficulties of this kind are evaluated in relation to a person's concerns. A loss that is irrecoverable, particularly of a close relationship, will cause separation anxiety and deep sadness – damage to the social motivational systems of attachment and/or affiliation. Humiliations add a dimension of shame. Entrapment means being unable to do anything about the problem (remember Epictetus' idea of what is and is not in a person's power to change). Danger is a prediction that causes anxiety that things will remain bad or get worse.

Some 30 percent of Brown and Harris's sample suffered severe life events or difficulties but did not become depressed. Why was this? The second major result the authors found was a set of factors that either protected a woman from adversity or made her vulnerable to it.

The most important protective factor is known in social and health science as social support. Among the women in Brown and Harris's study this factor was represented by a woman having an intimate and affectionate relationship with at least one person, typically a spouse. If a severe adversity occurred, a woman who had a supportive relationship was far less likely to become depressed or clinically anxious than someone who did not have such a relationship.

Vulnerability factors have opposite effects. They make people more likely to become depressed. They include childhood adversities of various kinds, including loss of a mother before the age of 11. As research following Brown and Harris has proceeded, it has become clear that vulnerability to depression is complex. For instance, genes can make one vulnerable in several ways, including effects on the probability of adversities occurring, and difficulties in establishing social support.[10] For some people, also, episodes of depression have a kindling effect, with each episode of depression increasing the risk of becoming depressed again subsequently, even in the absence of a provoking stress or adversity.[11]

A Very Brief History of Psychiatry

The specialty of psychiatry is the medical practice of caring for people with emotional disorders, and with disturbances of the mind and of behavior. The term "psychiatrist" means something like attendant to the soul. The shape of psychiatric practice, as a branch of medicine, was set by the end of the nineteenth century,[12] when Emil Kraepelin brought out a new edition of his textbook of psychiatry[13] in which he divided psychiatric illnesses into 13 groups. Along with such classifications as mental retardation was febrile psychosis (psychosis caused by fever), which could have been his diagnosis of the woman from Thasos. Two classifications in Kraepelin's book attracted great attention. They were called functional psychoses because they had no obvious cause in any recognized medical condition. One was manic-depressive psychosis. The other was dementia praecox (dementia that happens early in life rather than towards its end), which later came to be called schizophrenia.

The idea of functional psychoses that are not caused by recognized conditions such as brain damage, fever, or other physical illnesses, or in modern days the use of so-called "recreational drugs," has continued. At the same time these psychoses have some characteristics of physical illness. Among their distinguishing features is that the patients are typically deluded: they have periods when they have no awareness that certain of their thoughts and moods that seem bizarre to others are anything but realistic. Such conditions are alarming to those who know the sufferer.

According to Kraepelin's classification, manic-depressive illness (now also called bipolar disorder) was the less severe of the two functional psychoses, because patients often recovered. It is a disturbance of the emotions. The prototypical patient alternates between periods of mania (being excitable, happy, speeding through life, acting on impulse) and periods of deep depression.

By contrast, schizophrenic patients display what is usually called emotional blunting, and seem not to react to events or people in the usual emotional ways. They have symptoms of classic kinds of madness, such as hallucinations of voices commenting on their every action, or the deeply held conviction that malign powers are controlling their thoughts or body.

In former times, psychoses seemed to demand hospitalization. Asylums built on the edges of cities were in the twentieth century renamed mental hospitals. They were places in which patients with psychoses were contained. The reputation gained by schizophrenia as a chronic deteriorating condition often had much to do with its sufferers being institutionalized. Another legacy of Kraepelin was to see psychoses as having genetic bases. This idea has been largely borne out by studies of twins and adoption. In both manic-depressive illness and schizophrenia, if one member of an identical twin pair has a diagnosis of the illness, the chance is more than 50 percent that the other twin (with the same genes) will have the illness too. By contrast, a twin who does not share the same genes as his or her non-identical psychotic twin brother or sister will have a much lower chance of having the same illness. There are also genetic risks for depression and anxiety states,[14] but they are far less severe than for psychoses.

The descendant of Kraepelin's classificatory work is the American Psychiatric Association's *Diagnostic and statistical manual of mental disorders*, which has become standard world-wide, and is now in its fourth edition known as *DSM-IV*.[15] Just as Kraepelin described 13 kinds of psychiatric disorder, the *DSM-IV* team had 13 work groups, each composed of experts who reviewed research literature and practice for a particular set of disorders (anxiety disorders, eating disorders, mood disorders, which include depression, schizophrenia, and so on) and wrote the corresponding section of the manual.

Kraepelin's contemporary, Sigmund Freud, had his main effect on how neuroses were seen. By comparison with psychoses, which are relatively rare, one may think of neuroses as states we are all likely to suffer: anxieties in their many forms, obsessions, addictions of various kinds, sexual dysfunctions, eating disorders, hostilities, depressions. One may think of them as states on a normal dimension of personality, Neuroticism, which was discussed in the previous chapter. Freud proposed that neurotic disorders might be resolved by his form of therapy: psychoanalysis.[16] If, for people in the tradition of Kraepelin, psychotic disorders were genetically based medical illnesses, for people influenced by Freud and his followers, neurotic disorders were problems in living. Their causes were thought to be in inner conflicts derived from childhood relationships, principally with parents.

In recent decades the mental hospitals that were once asylums have been closed, partly because of the intellectual climate, which condemned involuntary institutionalization, but also because drugs became available to control mood, behavior, and thought-patterns in psychotic conditions. At the same time, governmental health authorities throughout Europe and North America have wanted to save money and have people looked after, as the idea has it, "in the community." Hence the people one can now see on street corners yelling at someone who is not there.

If someone now has an episode of psychosis, that person will most likely be seen by a psychiatrist as an out-patient. And if he or she is hospitalized to stabilize a drug treatment plan, this will often be in the psychiatric ward of a general hospital. And rather than keeping the patient in hospital for a long time, the medical staff will be keen to have the drugs working well enough for the patient to be discharged from hospital as soon as possible.

The New Epidemiology

There were several revolutionary features of Brown and Harris's study of women's depression. One was that the researchers did not study principally the people who had previously provided the main material for psychiatric research: those patients in mental hospitals who had the exotic symptoms of madness. The newer researchers' principal samples were of ordinary people in the community. In this way, Brown and Harris found that a large proportion of women who had a first onset of depression broke down for reasons that were comprehensible in their lives.

Although not so glamorous or daring as brain surgery, the findings of epidemiology are fundamental. The first insights into a scientific basis of physical medicine, the origins of infectious diseases of the kind that caused fevers, were epidemiological, and they began in the middle of the nineteenth century. Cholera was found to be transmitted by dirty water,[17] and carried by self-reproducing organisms that we now call bacteria. Although one might think that the really big advance in the medicine of infectious diseases came with the discovery of antibiotics, this is not so. Antibiotics are undoubtedly important, but they did not become available until the 1940s. The largest effects on the human war on micro-organisms began 70 years earlier with public health measures that provided clean water, disposed of sewage safely, removed garbage, and alerted people to the importance of preserving and cooking food carefully. These measures sharply reduced the incidence of infectious diseases and improved health so much that populations began to grow enormously throughout the industrialized world. Comparably, the introduction of drugs that relieved anxiety (such as Valium), anti-depressants (such as Prozac), which relieved some of the most despairing moods of depression, and anti-psychotic drugs (such as Largactil), which reduced symptoms of schizophrenia and mania, has been undoubtedly important. But it has been work on the epidemiology of emotional disorders that has solved the main problems of what such disorders are, how they are caused, and what might be done about them preventatively.

Table 7.1 gives results from a recent study of 8,098 people in USA, by Ronald Kessler and his team, who used interviews to make diagnoses. They linked diagnoses to aspects of each person's life, such as sex, income, race, living place. The figures in the table, called lifetime prevalences, indicate the proportion of the people in the population who have suffered from each kind of disorder at any time in their life. For some kinds of disorder – for example, major depression – this will often be a single episode; for others – for example, alcoholism – the condition will typically have occupied a person for a large part of his or her life; for yet others – for example, anti-social personality disorder – the condition may have lasted a lifetime.

The first line of the table shows that major depression occurs about 1.7 times more frequently in women than in men. The next line, "manic episode," includes people who would be diagnosed

Table 7.1 Percentages of adults in the 48 contiguous states of the USA who have suffered each kind of psychiatric condition in their lifetime

Disorder	Male	Female	Total
Affective (depression-related) disorder			
Major depressive episode	12.7	21.3	17.1
Manic episode	1.6	1.7	1.6
Dysthymia	4.8	8.0	6.4
Any affective disorder	14.7	23.9	19.3
Anxiety disorders			
Panic disorder	2.0	5.0	3.5
Agoraphobia without panics	3.5	7.0	5.3
Social phobia	11.1	15.5	13.3
Simple phobia	6.7	15.7	11.3
Generalized anxiety disorder	3.6	6.6	5.1
Any anxiety disorder	19.2	30.5	24.9
Other disorders			
Alcohol or drug abuse or dependence	35.4	17.9	26.6
Anti-social personality	5.8	1.2	3.5
Non-affective psychosis	0.6	0.8	0.7
Any psychiatric disorder	48.7	47.3	48.0

Source: Kessler et al. (1994).

with manic-depressive (or bipolar) illness. Dysthymia is a condition of low mood that is less serious than major depression.

Disorders in the next block, "clinical anxiety," are again more common in women than men (1.6 to 1), with the most serious of these conditions, panics and agoraphobia, social phobia, and generalized anxiety disorder, making it difficult for people to function in the world. Simple phobias, for instance of spiders, or heights, are not uncommon, but although they may restrict the sufferer to some extent, they tend not to be generally disabling.

The first line in the last block shows that men are approximately twice as likely as women to suffer alcohol and drug abuse and dependence. Anti-social personality disorder is almost five times as common in men as in women. People with this diagnosis are often angry, aggressive, and do harm to others; they include people of the kind described by Jenkins as having an anger organization and of the kind followed up from age 8 to 38 by Caspi and his colleagues,[18] discussed in the previous chapter. One may say that they have put together the social emotion of anger with the anti-social emotion of contempt for others. Many with this disorder will have spent time in prison. The last line of the block, of non-affective psychosis, is largely of people with schizophrenia.

The very last line of the table is a summary. Almost half of all Americans – and the figures are similar for other Western industrialized countries – will at some time in their lives have suffered from a psychiatric disorder.

Perhaps the most striking finding of this study is that income makes a huge difference. People were one-and-a-half times more likely to have suffered depression, and twice as likely to have suffered anxiety disorder, if they had (in the 1990s) a family income of $19,000 a year or less as compared with a family income of $70,000 or more. Money is a resource. To the extent to which emotional and other psychiatric disorders are affected by slings and arrows of fortune, those with more resources can often cope with them better. Also, however, those who suffer from disorders are often less able to earn a good living.

Genes and Environment

A big puzzle in the understanding of emotional disorders has been why, in children and adults who have a history of experiencing the same stress, some suffer a disorder, and some do not. Protective factors such as social support, and vulnerability factors such as the loss of a parent during childhood, are possible reasons, but not a complete explanation. I indicated in the previous chapter that genes affect temperament, and in this chapter that they affect psychoses, and to a lesser extent anxiety and depression. But how do they have such effects?

The new millennium has ushered in an understanding of the human genome. Genes were discovered in 1903. Exactly fifty years later Watson and Crick proposed that genetic information was carried by four chemical substances, called bases (adenine, thymine, guanine, and cytosine), which act like letters in an alphabet or code.[19] In 2001, a first draft of all 3 billion letters of a sequence of the human DNA code was published. This achievement has opened new opportunities to answer questions about genetic vulnerability.

Each cell in our bodies carries the whole code for an individual. It is not identical for each of us. There is no single human sequence, any more than everyone has the same fingerprint. There is both sameness – what it is to be human – and variation. Variations make each of us male or female, tall or short, and with a distinctively recognizable face.

A gene is a sequence of DNA code. Though the whole human genome has been mapped, and some genes have been identified, we are a long way from knowing what each gene does. It is not even known how many active genes there are. In the whole genome, only about 2 percent of the DNA is thought to be active genes; the number of genes in humans may be only about 30,000.

Genes carry the code that records the history of our species. They have been selected during our ancestors' adaptations to the world, as living beings, as animals, as vertebrates, as mammals, as primates, and as humans. Evolution also depends on variability, which Darwin saw as the raw material for natural selection. So chromosomes produce different versions of the human pattern.

How is the variability produced? In all the cells of the body except the egg and sperm, genes exist really as gene pairs, in two corresponding spots (loci) on 23 pairs of chromosomes. One set of 23 chromosomes came from our mother, from the egg, and the other set of 23 from our father, from the sperm that joined with the egg. Each gene in the chromosomes tends to come in a slightly different form, called an allele. Think of our chromosomes with paired genes as like a deck of cards that contain just spades and hearts (the different suits represent different alleles). Within this analogy, each parent hands over to an offspring one complete run (within the egg or sperm): Ace, 2, 3…Jack, Queen, King. Variability occurs because in the formation of eggs and sperm the paired cards are partially shuffled and each egg and sperm receives just one complete run (Ace to King) but with a variable set of hearts and spades. When the new individual is formed, the run from Ace to King from the egg will line up with the run from sperm, so the cells of the new individual again have two Aces, two 2's, and so on. Because of the shuffling, some of the pairs will be both hearts, some both spades, and some with one of each. Because shuffling is partial, some distinctive traits of the parents (derived from sequences of genes) are passed on to the offspring.

Genes and depression

At the dawn of the era of the genome, a study by Caspi, Sugden, Moffitt and their colleagues has thrown new light on the way in which genes and a history of the stress of life events combine to produce depression.[20] The researchers studied a large epidemiological sample of 1,032 people, members of the Dunedin Multidisciplinary Health and Development Study, in New Zealand (52 percent male, 48 percent female), who have been followed up at approximately two-year intervals since the age of 3. In the current study, they were aged 26. These people were assessed for how many stressful life events they had suffered between their 21st and 26th birthdays, and also tested for the 5HTT transporter gene, which promotes the transmitter substance serotonin. This gene was chosen for study because it affects serotonin in the ways discussed in Chapter 4.

The 5HTT transporter gene comes in two forms (alleles): a short form (s), and a long form (l). The long form is more efficient at promoting serotonin. On the relevant chromosome pairs, people might have two shorts (s/s) – in the Dunedin sample they were 17 percent of the population – a short and a long (s/l) – 51 percent in the Dunedin sample – or two longs (l/l) – 31 percent in the Dunedin sample.

The striking finding was that people who had suffered an adverse life event and had a short form of the 5HTT transporter gene in combination with the long form (s/l), and, with an even stronger effect, the double short (s/s), were more likely to become depressed than those with two copies of the long form (l/l). The short form of the 5HTT gene, in other words, produces less serotonin and is a vulnerability factor for depression. It had no effect on its own. It did, however, have an effect in making depression more likely when a severely stressful adversity occurred in a person's life.

With this study, Caspi and his colleagues have brought together understanding of how the genetic-biological-pharmaco-logical vulnerability to depression can interact with a history of adversities in the world to cause an episode of depression. All of us suffer adversities, and this book is built around the idea that many emotions signal to us that some problem has arisen in our lives which, even if it is not a severe adversity, challenges us to solve a problem. An adversity is a problem without much notice-able possibility of benefit to our purposes in life. In depression one has lost hope of any solution.

Most depressions do resolve. For most people, the adversity passes. Some people start new plans, new relationships.[21] For others, it is as if forces of re-evaluation with which depression presses us finally lead to a solution. This may involve re-evaluat-ing who one is or what one is doing in life. Depression can be disabling. When it is thought about in certain ways, however – perhaps ways of the kind that the Epicureans and Stoics pro-posed – it can also be the occasion for a new start. In terms of the idea of emotions as challenges (see Chapter 2) and of dynamic systems (Chapter 6), a seriously adverse life event and its emo-tions can challenge us in the most stringent way. One path forward might derive from wisdom and enable us to learn;[22] another might be merely a route to giving up.

Against the world

One of the most urgent and widely researched matters of mental health is why some children grow up to be classified as having anti-social personality disorder, often with convictions for violent offenses, and spend substantial parts of their adult life in prison, while others from similar backgrounds lead peaceable and more contented lives.

In his original work on attachment, Bowlby thought that being raised without a consistently loving mother would lead to a child becoming an affectionless psychopath. This was a good pointer, but the prediction was too pessimistic. Subsequent evidence indicates that two kinds of early environments tend to produce continuingly aggressive people. One is a style of ineffective family management, studied mainly in the families of boys, that encourages the boys to acquire scripts of yelling, hitting, and temper tantrums, which enable them to get their own way by aggressive coercion. These increase the likelihood of a continuing anger organization, and careers as anti-social personalities.[23] A second path involves a stressful home environment in which there has been physical maltreatment and abuse. Some children have both a cooercive script and a history of maltreatment.

It was to the second path (of childhood maltreatment) that Caspi and his colleagues devoted another study of gene–environment interactions.[24] They found that, as with the effects of stress on depression, the effects of maltreatment of children do not fall with the same weight on everyone who experiences them. They studied the same Dunedin cohort discussed in the previous section. For each person in the cohort, they tested for different forms of a gene that promotes monoamine oxidase. Genetic deficiency in this enzyme has been linked with depression in both mice and humans.

Caspi and his colleagues tested for the two forms of the Mono-Amine Oxidase A (MAOA) gene. Monoamine oxidase is an enzyme that deactivates a set of amine-based transmitter substances. The gene is located on the X chromosome. Males have an X and a Y chromosome, with the Y being much shorter in length. Thus in boys, genes on most of the X chromosome cannot be moderated by genes on the other chromosome, and the MAOA gene is of this kind.

Although there was no association between presence of the gene for low MAOA activity and a history of maltreatment in childhood, those with the low MAOA form of the gene who had been maltreated in childhood were far more likely to grow up with significant symptoms of aggressive violence than those who had the higher MAOA form of the gene who had also been maltreated. Although those with the gene for low MAOA activity who had also suffered maltreatment were only 12 percent of the population of boys in the cohort, they were responsible for 44 percent of the cohort's convictions for violent crime. Some 85 percent of the boys with the low MAOA gene who were severely maltreated developed some form of anti-social behavior.

Girls with the low MAOA gene were also susceptible. Of the 481 females in the sample, only 2 percent had convictions for violence. This was insufficient for statistical analyses of violent crimes, but behavior was analyzed. Girls with the low MAOA gene on either X chromosome were more likely to show delinquent behavior during adolescence. The fact that the MAOA genes acted in the same kind of way in girls as they did in boys was significant. But being female and having two X chromosomes allowed a normal MAOA gene on one chromosome to moderate the vulnerability effect of the low MAOA gene on the other, and thereby conferred substantial protection from its potentially harmful effects. Investigating further along this route, we may come to understand what is perhaps the most important but least understood fact about violent acts: why men are so much more likely than women to commit them.

CHAPTER EIGHT

Emotional Intelligence

What Is It to be Emotionally Intelligent? Are There Skills to Learn?

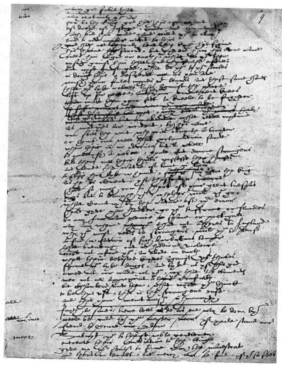

Part of a manuscript page from The play of Sir Thomas More, on which Shakespeare worked with several other playwrights. This is the only surviving example of dramatic work in Shakespeare's own handwriting. Source: British Library (British Library Harley MS 7368 f.9).

Emotions and Us

Although Shakespeare's handwriting is not easy to read – it was in what is known as an Elizabethan secretary hand – his words and their usages are the bases of the English we speak today. For him and other English writers of the Renaissance, "intelligence" meant understanding.[1] "Emotion" is a newer term, scarcely used until 200 years ago. Before that there were passions, sentiments, feelings, affections. Such words occupied a cluster that included sin, will, grace, soul.[2] By contrast, "emotion" is a term from literary and scientific clusters that became prevalent only during the nineteenth century. These clusters include other terms such as expression, nerves, viscera, and brain.

Along with offering a definition, most modern dictionaries remark that emotion is often contrasted with logic, or with rationality, or with cognition. Such remarks derive from folk theory. In Western cultures, we tend to believe that intelligence and emotion are at odds. With this sense of inner contradiction, what might the term "emotional intelligence" mean? Peter Salovey and his friend Jack Mayer coined the term some fifteen years ago, as Salovey recounted,[3] when Mayer was helping him paint a room in the Salovey house. A few years later it was an idea whose time was come. The idea is that emotional intelligence is a distinctive faculty of understanding that enables us to recognize our own emotions and those of others so that we can manage our lives and relationships.

In 1995, the term "emotional intelligence" was used by *New York Times* journalist Daniel Goleman, as the title of a book. Though Goleman acknowledges Salovey and Mayer, he went rather further than they did to propose that emotional intelligence can determine our health and our success in life. These claims seem extravagant, but we cannot yet assess them. Instead, while I discuss some relevant studies towards the end of the chapter, mostly I approach this very new subject historically, tracing aspects of the idea of emotional intelligence from the Renaissance to the twentieth century.

Four Branches of Emotional Intelligence

Mayer and Salovey propose that emotional intelligence has four aspects that they call branches,[4] as follows:

- Branch 1: Perceiving emotion.
- Branch 2: Using emotions to facilitate thought.
- Branch 3: Understanding emotions.
- Branch 4: Managing emotions.

The twist that Mayer and Salovey put on the implications of the preceding 40 years of research on emotions was to start with distinct areas in which there had been good progress, and to conceptualize people's emotional abilities as skills in these areas. IQ (Intelligence Quotient) is believed by many of those who do research on it to be genetically fairly fixed: you are endowed with an IQ of 75, or 100, or 125 or whatever it may be. Some researchers tend to think that EQ may also be of this kind.[5] But by analyzing emotional intelligence into skills, Mayer, Salovey and their colleagues enable one to see how one might improve.

Perceiving emotion

The first set of abilities named by Mayer and Salovey includes the following examples:

- the ability to identify emotion in oneself;
- the ability to identify emotion in others, as well as in stories and films;
- the ability to express emotions and emotional needs accurately;
- the ability to tell the difference between honest and dishonest emotions.

Knowing one's own emotions   Often we know what causes our emotions, and there does not seem much to be intelligent about. But when we look beneath the surface, some of our emotions become more challenging and as fascinating as anything you will read about in a mystery story. "Yes," you might say, "I know I'm angry at him. It's because he let me down. But why *so* angry? And why does it take over my mind for stretches of time? And what would it take for the anger to dissipate?" Or: "I know I'm very attracted, but why to that person?" As we try to understand our emotions, what had seemed straightforward turns out not to be.

Joanna Field did brilliant detective work on her emotions. She had been a psychology student at the University of London in the 1920s. She found herself wondering what the conditions for happiness in her life might be. As an experiment, she decided to keep a diary of episodes of happiness and what led to them.[6] When she started, she thought that within a few weeks she would be able to say: "these are the facts of my life, now I'm going to do something about it." She wrote: "If it should turn out that happiness did not matter, I should have a chance of finding out what was more important."[7] Things did not turn out as she expected. One morning, she found her main concern had been whether she could get her hair cut before going to work. The rest of the day was just as banal. She found herself worrying about what people at work thought of her hair-cut.

Field became more and more perplexed. She had thought she organized her life rationally, but wrote that "whichever of [her] aims might be the most important to work for," she would get nowhere because her life was not determined by any one aim, but by "a plan-less mixture of all of them."[8]

> I wanted many friends, but had often refused invitations because I hated to feel the beautiful free space of an empty day ... broken by social obligations. I had thought I wanted to be a unique individual, but had been filled with shame when someone disagreed with me ... I wanted to be importantly useful in the world but avoided all opportunities for responsibility.[9]

Field discovered that much of her life was determined by what she called "blind thoughts," which took directions of their own and left trails of upsets, worries, and bad moods. Here, for instance, is something that Field wrote about a person who was much better off than herself:

> Oughtn't we to invite those people in for tea. That's best, say "Do you ever have time for a cup of tea?" ... will the maid open the door? will she be too busy? what shall we give them? go into town

to buy a cake? will they expect it? can't afford these extras but bread and jam won't do.[10]

In this anxious little train of thoughts, Joanna Field worries about how to approach a wealthy person. She worries about being unused to dealing with a servant. She worries that she will be rejected ("will she be too busy?"), worries that she will feel ashamed of what she can offer. She had been aware of her moods, but their origin in the chatter of her anxieties was unsuspected. The blind thoughts hovered at the edge of her consciousness. Only when she wrote them in a diary could she see them for what they were: the causes of her bad moods. She concluded that they were like thoughts of a child, of a 6-year-old stuck at an early stage of development, self-absorbed, worrying about petty issues and about what others might think. They are the same kinds of thoughts that had been considered by the Stoics and early Christians, and that were rediscovered decades after Field's book by Tim Beck, the founder of cognitive behavioral therapy. He found they were responsible for clinically significant anxieties and depressions (see the episode of the medical records librarian described in Chapter 3).

For every act that was prompted by a rational decision, Field found dozens that grew out of her self-absorbed reverie. Because her anxious trains of thoughts had not been acknowledged, they were insulated from the real world, from other people, or from her own guidance. She found her anxiously chattering mind was a mean mind. It set impossible standards, and was scornful of her when she did not live up to them.

At last, after years of investigation, Field made a discovery within herself of a more secure basis for living. She wrote:

In the end my deliverance came suddenly . . . the idea occurred to me that until you have, once at least, faced everything that you know – the whole universe – with utter giving in, and let all that is "not you" flow over and engulf you, there can be no lasting sense of security.[11]

She realized that her fears were of being disliked, criticized, of being taken over by others, and that without realizing it, fears and anxieties of this kind had been a fundamental influence in her life.

I realized now that as long as you feel insecure you have no real capacity to face other men and women in that skill of communication which more than any other skill requires freedom from tension...I was now finding that I chiefly reckoned each day's catch of happiness in terms of my relationships with others.

Perceiving other people's emotions   Mayer and Salovey proposed that there is a distinct ability to perceive emotions in others. Starting in the 1960s, Paul Ekman and Wallace Friesen found that certain facial expressions that signified specific emotions – happiness, sadness, anger, fear, surprise, and disgust – are recognized worldwide.[12]

Ekman and O'Sullivan have shown that even when people try to avoid giving off clues about their emotions, for instance when lying, some facial expressions – notably anxiety – leak out.[13] Such micro-expressive leakages last only a fraction of a second, and most people do not perceive them. Ekman has trained law enforcement personnel to detect them, and in his recent book,[14] he gives advice to readers about how to recognize emotions in facial expressions more generally. This is a skill, however, that is severely restricted among people with certain kinds of damage to the amygdala (discussed in Chapter 4), who can recognize who a person is by his or her face, but find it difficult to recognize certain emotional expressions at all.[15]

Recognizing emotions depends on many more kinds of cues than facial expressions. Sally Planalp and her colleagues have identified several kinds, each of which can be used alone or in combination; these include tones of voice, gestures, actions, what people say, and what they don't say.[16] Knowing what someone is feeling also depends on how well you know that person, so specific skills may not be the whole answer. If you wanted to check your knowledge of someone else's emotions, ask a partner, room-mate, or friend to keep an emotion diary during times when you are together. Your friend or partner keeps a diary of his or her own emotions. You keep a diary for that person's emotions that you notice. Then compare notes.

Using emotions to facilitate thought

Here is Mayer and Salovey's list of exemplary abilities in this area:

- the ability to direct thinking on the basis of emotions;
- the ability to imagine emotions in order to remember and make judgments;
- the ability to use mood swings to appreciate several different points of view;
- the ability to use emotions to help creativity and to solve problems.

Mood and thought   Emotions affect what we think about and how we think. If we treat them aright, they can be gateways to accomplishment. Everyone who has used a deadline to get started in writing a paper or preparing a presentation has used an emotion – fear – to get his or her thoughts going. Every person in sales or in public relations knows that giving a customer a small gift, which makes them mildly happy, inclines them towards positive judgments of a product. Not everyone, however, knows that being happy rather than not happy is conducive to creative problem solving. Alice Isen was the first to do experiments in which she induced moods to investigate their cognitive and interpersonal effects. She and two colleagues[17] gave people, one at a time, a box of tacks, a book of matches, and a candle, and asked each to attach the candle to a cork-board wall and light it so that it would burn without dripping wax on the table or floor. Substantially more people who were made mildly happy by watching a comedy film, or by being given candy, solved the problem than those who were in a neutral mood. In this task, it is impossible to fix the candle directly to the corkboard using the tacks. The tacks are not long enough, and they just break the candle wax. The solution is to pour the tacks out of the box, and pin the box's tray to the corkboard so that it functions as a shelf for the candle, which could then be put on the shelf and lit. The effect of the positive mood was large, about the same as starting the person off in the task with the tacks already poured out of the box onto the table so the tray was empty and suggestive of its use as a shelf. In general, then, if you need to be creative, a happy mood will help.

Other research has shown that happy moods enable positive memories to come to mind, whereas negative moods tend to elicit negative memories. In one study,[18] people had a positive or negative mood induced by giving them problems and telling them either that they had been successful or that they had been unsuccessful. They were then given a standard set of questions and asked to use them to interview a candidate for a job. The candidate was a confederate of the experimenter. He or she followed a script and would answer each question with three positive and three negative pieces of information about himself or herself. For instance, in answer to the question, "What are your most important traits?" the candidate would say, "I'm ambitious and reliable, Also I'm pretty friendly. On the minus side, some of my friends tell me I'm pretty stubborn and I know I'm impatient. Also I'm pretty disorganized." The interviewers in whom a negative mood had been induced by telling them they were unsuccessful in their problem task remembered many more of the negative things and tended not to recommend the candidate for the job. Those in whom a positive mood had been induced remembered the positive responses, and did recommend the candidate.

Most professionals seem to do better at their jobs by being in positive moods, since these moods encourage cooperation. But anxiety is a mood that is conducive for being systematic, and checking for mistakes. Being a lawyer, as it turns out, is one of the few professions in which a tone of negative emotions predominates, and can be helpful: a lawyer's job includes looking out for everything that could possibly go wrong.[19]

Understanding emotions

Mayer and Salovey's examples of skills of understanding are as follows:

- the ability to understand how one emotion may relate to others;
- the ability to know how emotions are caused and what can follow from them;
- the ability to understand mixtures of different emotions;
- the ability to understand how one emotion can change to another.

We recognize the Renaissance as the beginning of the modern European world. Among the famous people of that time was Erasmus: the first person to make wide use of the invention of printing for secular purposes. The invention helped to distribute his writings. His most famous book, then and now, was *Praise of Folly*, written in 1509. In it, Folly stands up and makes a speech in praise of herself: a very foolish thing to do:

> ... it's admitted [she says] that all the emotions belong to Folly, and this is what marks the wise man off from the fool; he is ruled by reason, the fool by his emotions. ... But in fact these emotions not only act as guides to those hastening towards the haven of wisdom, but also wherever virtue is put into practice they are always present to act like spurs and goads as incentives to good deeds.[20]

Praise of Folly is in parts a parody of those who believe they are ruled by reason, but when looked at from the outside appear to be driven by emotions that are foolish and trivial. Sometimes Folly satirizes Erasmus's own scholarly activities, which might appear to be of this kind. In the end, she says that fools, simple people affected by emotions, are the wisest of all. They have often been able to live lives of kindness, while those who are self-importantly proud of their own wisdom have not.

Shakespeare is considered the most important writer in English, and one can think of the Renaissance coming to its end with his death in 1616. He was a bookish person, and it is known that he read Erasmus.[21] It seems certain therefore that he read *Praise of Folly*. It is likely, I believe, that it was this book which took him to a turning point and enabled him to conceive his greatest plays. One can imagine him reading, or re-reading, this satirical book, with its contrasts between surface behavior and inner substance, which includes emotions, around 1594 and having the following thought. To understand the behavior of people in love, or what goes on in politics, it is no good saying love is blind or politicians are self-serving. These are clichés. No insight occurs, nothing changes. One must move the matter onto a different plane, perhaps satire, like Folly praising herself, or perhaps in some other way that will allow us to understand both surface and substance, and the relation between them. Shakespeare's plays from about 1594 onwards are his use of the theater to enable understandings of emotions in this new way.

As to love, around 1595 Shakespeare wrote *A midsummer night's dream*, in which people fall in love for reasons they don't comprehend. This is represented by the mischievous Puck instilling the juice of "a little Western flower" into the eyes of a someone sleeping. On waking, he or she falls in love with the first person seen. And when such newly-in-love people talk, they are eloquent about why they love just this particular individual. It is the emotion, love, that sets up the relationship. What people in the play say about their love is the outward and public talk that articulates the substance of their inward and personal feeling. (One might compare the effect with the peptides and other substances that change emotions, discussed in Chapter 4.)

As to politics, Shakespeare made the daring move of juxtaposing the plotting of lordly politicians with scoundrels. So *Henry IV Part I* opens with King Henry saying that now various uprisings in the country have been quelled, the English can go and attack foreigners: go on a crusade against the Turks. But as he is talking, news comes that Hotspur has just won a good battle, and secured a large ransom. Henry turns his aggressive attention from a foreign crusade towards yet more wars at home. The scene that immediately follows is of a group of layabouts at the tavern, who include the King's son, Hal, and his indolent companion, Falstaff, who plan an armed robbery of a group of pilgrims. To write a play in which lordly aggression is juxtaposed with roguish robbery is allows us to see national and international politics in a fresh way.

Shakespeare's emotional intelligence was sufficiently acute to prompt us constantly beyond our own current understandings. His most famous play is *Hamlet*. Briefly, its main plot-line is as follows. Claudius has become King on the death of his brother, and he has married Hamlet's mother, Gertrude. Hamlet, the son of the dead king, is visited by the ghost of his father, who tells him that he was murdered by Claudius. Hamlet vows revenge. He stages a play to depict Claudius's guilt, and observe his reaction to the performance. After it, Hamlet goes to talk with his mother in her private rooms. While he is there, he hears someone hidden behind a tapestry, and, thinking him to be Claudius, he stabs him to death. The person turns out to be Polonius, the Kings counselor. Polonius's son, Laertes, vows revenge on Hamlet. Claudius arranges that Hamlet and Laertes fight a duel in which Hamlet's rapier has a button at the end, to prevent wounding, while Laertes's rapier is sharp and poisoned. Hamlet is wounded. In a scuffle, the rapiers change hands.

Laertes is wounded, and tells Hamlet that Claudius has rigged the fencing match, whereon Hamlet runs Claudius through with the poisoned rapier.

The real movement of the play does not, however, take place via its plot. It takes place in its emotions and their transformations, which run in what one may think of as emotion line through the play and form its center, as sometimes music, lighting, and atmosphere form the central thread of a film.[22]

Hamlet starts with anxiety: what is the meaning of the ghost that has been seen on the castle ramparts? This anxiety engages the audience, and is seamlessly transformed into another emotion: identification with angry vengefulness when Hamlet hears from the ghost that his uncle has killed his father. We, the audience, eagerly join Hamlet in identification with this vengefulness. When Hamlet kills Polonius, the emotion line of angry vengeance splits in two, so that the original line is accompanied by its mirror image. Hamlet the avenger is now also Hamlet the guilty one, target of another's revenge. As Hamlet says of Laertes:

> For by the image of my cause I see
> The portraiture of his[23]

The emotional center-point of the play is reached when Hamlet visits his mother in her private rooms. After he has killed Polonius by mistake, he confronts Gertrude with what she has done in marrying his uncle. He does not tell her that he has evidence that her former husband was killed by her new husband. Everything takes place at the level of emotions. He expresses disgust at her sexual activity with Claudius. This causes Gertrude to feel intense shame. As she repents, the next transformation occurs. She emotionally deserts Claudius and re-establishes her attachment relationship with her son. It is a moving moment at the very center of the play. Although by killing Polonius, in terms of the plot Hamlet has lost all influence on events and is sent away to England, emotionally he is empowered: "The readiness is all."[24] As the play nears its end, we the audience are profoundly moved by Hamlet's death. Our sadness on his behalf then transforms to a compassion for all of us, humankind, subject to such fits of anger and vengefulness in which by identification we have willingly taken part, and by which destruction occurs that we do not will.

So, although a great deal of effort, by the Stoics and others, has been devoted to considering how thought may transform emotion, perhaps Shakespeare gets closer to the truth with his idea that it is emotion that transforms emotion. Two generations after Shakespeare, Baruch Spinoza wrote that an "emotion can only be controlled or destroyed by another emotion contrary thereto, and with more power for controlling emotion."[25] This does not contradict the idea of re-evaluation, but describes how it can occur.

Managing emotions

Here are Mayer and Salovey's examples:

- the ability to be open to emotions, both pleasant and unpleasant;
- the ability to follow the course of one's own emotions, and reflect on them;
- the ability to engage in, prolong, or detach from an emotional state;
- the ability to manage emotions in oneself;
- the ability to manage emotions in others.

In medieval times in Europe the seven deadly sins were widely known. I discussed them in Chapter 3: gluttony, lust, avarice, envy, anger, sloth, and pride. They are emotional states to which we humans are subject: states we should avoid, though often we cannot. Set against them are more benificent emotions such as hope and fortitude, first among which is love. Love was thought to flow from God: the principle that formed the world from chaos, and which enabled society to flourish. Sins were destructive because they threatened to return the world to primeval chaos. We can see the idea of sin as an injunction to manage certain negative emotions.

Renaissance exhortations   Among the best known paintings of the Renaissance are two by Sandro Botticelli, *Primavera* and *Venus rising from the waves*. They were painted about 1477–8 for the villa of a member of the wealthy Medici banking family, the adolescent Lorenzo di Pierfrancesco de' Medici. Botticelli worked with Marsilio Ficino, the leading literary figure in Florence at the time, who was tutor to the young Lorenzo.[26] To accompany the painting of the *Primavera*, Ficino wrote to his young charge:

> The astrologers have it that he is the happiest man for whom Fate has so disposed the heavenly signs that Luna [the moon] is in no bad aspect to Mars and Saturn, that furthermore she is in favourable aspect to Sol [the sun] and Jupiter, Mercury and Venus.... We must not look for these matters outside ourselves, for all the heavens are within us and the fiery vigour in us testifies to our heavenly origin.... Onward then, great-minded youth ... dispose your own heavens.[27]

Astrology derived from the ancient Babylonian scientists, who sought to understand the relation of external events to ourselves. Ficino describes how the young man should not regard himself as subject to fates determined by external objects, the stars. He should understand that he is moved by emotions with all their fiery vigor (Mars – aggression; Saturn – melancholy; Venus – love; and so forth), and that he should dispose them within himself. He should, says Ficino, fix the eye of his soul

> ... on Venus herself, that is to say on Humanity ... a nymph of excellent comeliness born of heaven and more than others beloved of God all highest. Her soul and mind are Love and Charity ... if you were to unite with her in wedlock and claim her as yours she would make all your years sweet and make you the father of fine children.[28]

Botticelli's paintings depict Venus, visualized so that the young Lorenzo could contemplate her. In the revolutionary thinking of the Renaissance, Venus the Graeco-Roman lust-goddess is transformed into Christian "Love and Charity" (humanity), the basis of a worthwhile life. Botticelli's *Primavera* shows Venus, with head slightly inclined, walking towards the viewer. On her left are the three Graces and Mercury. On her right is Flora strewing flowers, and a nymph (perhaps a different aspect of Venus) being pursued by the wind. The other painting that accompanied this one, of Venus rising on a giant conch shell from the waves, has a similar theme.

The idea is sown that we humans need not passively accept what is in the stars, or, as we might now say, in our genes. We can arrange our emotions at least to some extent, come to know them, integrate them into our character and our life. In a relationship of care, Ficino and Botticelli sought to teach their student, at the threshold of adult sexuality, to arrange his emotions within himself. They offered him a gift that made the principal emotion, love, herself beautiful, an object of inspiration. By recognizing love's beauty, and fixing the eye of his soul on her, the young man might more easily be able to lead a life of goodness and happiness.

Modern research: the pursuit of happiness Salovey and Mayer said in their original article on emotional intelligence: "Emotionally intelligent people may enhance their own and others' moods, and even manage emotions charismatically towards a worthwhile end."[29]

To reflect on experience is to enable oneself to learn from it, to be able to see how the disposal of one's emotions might occur in one's life. In more recent times Mihaly Csikszentmihalyi has taken Joanna Field's diary method a step further by giving people pagers and beeping them at random moments during the day. The people were asked, when the beeper sounded, to note where they were, what they were doing, and rate their mood on several scales. Csikszentmihalyi called the method experience sampling. From it derived important information on what kinds of things affected people's moods. This information was augmented by interviewing participants.[30]

We might think that being happy, or bitter, or anxious, will mostly be due to external events. And sometimes this is true, but Csikszentmihalyi found that while many people's emotions were taken over by the accidents of life, others conceived the world in a different way. This was illustrated by Rico Medelin, who worked on an assembly line in a factory that made movie projectors. The operation he had to do was supposed to take 43 seconds, and he had to do it nearly 600 times per day. Most of us would find this job stultifying. But Rico had worked at it for five years, and the samples of his experience were of happiness. He had turned his task into something like training for the Olympic Games. He had analyzed the task and worked out how to use his tools to become better and faster. His best average for the day was 28 seconds per unit. "It is better than anything else," said Rico. "It's better than watching TV."[31]

Rico had discovered a state of being that Csikszentmihalyi called "flow." Another participant, a 62-year-old woman who lived in the Italian Alps, found enjoyment in tending her cows and orchard. "I find a special satisfaction in caring for the plants," she said. "I like to see them grow each day."[32] A dancer described how it felt when a performance was going well: "Your concentration is very complete. Your mind isn't wandering, you are not thinking of something else; you are totally involved in what you are doing." A young mother with a small daughter said: "She reads to me, and I read to her, and that's a time when I sort of lose touch with the rest of the world. I'm totally absorbed in what I'm doing."

This state of flow, which Csikszentmihalyi also calls "optimal experience," is marked by a sense of creativity, of purpose, of people being fully engaged in what they are doing so that self and the activity merge. None of us has been able to choose aspects of our lives such as parents or siblings. By definition, the accidents of life are things we cannot affect. Some of us have little influence on where we live or how much we earn. As the Stoics found: we can't always influence the outer world, but we can influence our inner world. The modern message, however, is somewhat different: we can also choose to do what we are doing, turn it into a project in which we are engaged. Csikszentmihalyi summarizes the conditions for the state of flow. It is not a matter of waiting for the outside world to bring you pleasures. It's not watching television, or eating chocolate, or winning the lottery. You have to create for yourself meaningful activity. This involves a goal, problems to solve, skills that you learn, detailed feedback to evaluate how you are doing.

One of the great discoveries of cognitive psychology in recent years is that we can analyze what experts in any field are doing, then construct their understandings into something from which others can learn. This has happened in areas such as artistic activities and sports, and in learning to do particular jobs better. In the management of emotions, experts are people like Rico Medelin, and he is someone from whom we can learn. One won't get it right first time, or all the time. But as one's engagement in what one is doing increases, so will one's creativity and enjoyment.[33]

Measuring emotional intelligence

Among tests of emotional intelligence is one by Salovey and his colleagues: the MSCEIT (Mayer, Salovey, & Caruso Emotional

Intelligence Test). It measures distinct emotional skills based on the four branches of emotional intelligence, discussed above. For the first branch, "Perceiving emotions," people are given tasks of recognizing emotions in faces, paintings, and stories. The branch "Using emotions to facilitate thought" includes judgments of what kinds of tasks are best done in particular kinds of moods. For "Understanding emotions," questions include asking what emotions make up complex emotional states, like optimism. For "Managing emotions," people read scenarios and are asked about the effectiveness of alternative ways of handling the emotions that arise in them.

What does this test predict? It is new, so results are tentative, but in different studies higher emotional intelligence has been associated with reduced aggression in school children, less smoking and drinking in teenagers, and more effective performance among employees of an insurance company.[34] In particular, the fourth branch, "Managing emotions," which includes questions about how one might maintain good moods in oneself and how one maintain the emotional tone of one's relationships, has been promising. A question of this kind would be how one might maintain a warm friendship if there had been a large role change, for instance if one's friend had become one's boss. Higher scores on the scales of this branch have indeed been associated with good interactions with friends, as reported both by people taking the test and by their friends, even after IQ and the main personality traits have been accounted for.[35]

Conversation, Reading, Writing

I end this book with the idea from Shakespeare's time that intelligence means understanding. How may we understand our emotions? How should we manage them? This is not a self-help book. There are, however, personal practices as taught by Stoics, Yogis, Buddhist monks, and others, and there are practices that are helpful in developing understanding of the emotions of ourselves and others. Emotions do happen to us individually, and as such they can be observed and measured. More profoundly, in the history of understanding emotions, we continue rightly to distrust those emotions that are simply what Chrysippus would call first movements, and derive from what Keith Stanovich would identify as related to goals solely of our genes, rather than to goals of us as human beings. These include many of the instant urges of which wise people have been suspicious down the ages. We need to evaluate our evaluations. To help us in this, we can generally do no better than the traditional means: conversation, reading, and writing.

Conversation

Consider Robin Dunbar's book: *Grooming, gossip and the evolution of language*.[36] As I discussed in Chapter 5, grooming is a principal means by which affectionate relationships are maintained in primate groups. A corollary of Dunbar's evolutionary hypothesis of the increasing size of the primate brain with increased numbers of individuals in the social group is that as this number increased, so did the number of affectionate relationships one needed to maintain, and hence the amount of grooming one needed to do.

Primates need a third of their time for sleep, and a third of their time to travel and forage for food, so they can afford a maximum of a third of their time for grooming. But as group size increased towards human numbers, the time needed to maintain affectionate relationships exceeded this amount. The solution that Dunbar proposes was that, between a quarter-of- and half-a-million years ago in human pre-history, language emerged and enabled conversation to begin to take over the principal function of maintaining relationships. Conversation is verbal grooming. Though we never lose the important affectionate influence of touch, of cuddling, and other such ways of expressing emotions, language emerged to supplement them.[37] This adaptation enabled our forebears to maintain affectionate relationships among larger numbers of people. Conversation enables us not only to do something else, such as prepare food, while we verbally groom, it enables us to do it with more than one person at a time.[38] Perhaps most importantly, conversation, in its explicit commitments to other people, to joint plans, to shared beliefs, is in some ways more efficient in forming and maintaining relationships than manual grooming. In studies of what people talk about, Dunbar has found, indeed, that some 70 percent of it is about the social lives of ourselves and our acquaintances. These people are friends and enemies, the trusted and the untrustworthy. Dunbar has also proposed that music and laughter similarly function to promote social bonding: music when it is shared, as in group singing, is cohesive. Laughter bonds people together, perhaps by means that include the release of peptide substances in the brain called opioids.[39] Laughter and joking are important components of conversation; many people find it difficult to have close relationships with people with whom they cannot laugh.

Next one might read Theodore Zeldin's delightful little book *Conversation*, in which he writes:

> Humans have already changed the world several times by changing the way they have had conversations. There have been conversational revolutions which have been as important as wars and riots and famine. When problems have appeared insoluble, when life has seemed to be meaningless, when governments have been powerless, people have sometimes found a way out by changing the subject of their conversation, or the way they talked, or the persons they talked to. In the past that has given us the Renaissance, the Enlightenment, modernity and postmodernity. Now it's time for the New Conversation.[40]

The New Conversation, I think, will carry more awareness of its roots in affectionate relationships, and become more alive, perhaps, to the idea that emotions are the roots of relationships. If emotions are primarily social commitments, to concentrate on them is to concentrate on our relationships. To allow emotions importance as compared with reason as Folly recommended in Erasmus's book, is to consider that relationships are important rather than, in a solitary way, merely thinking what to believe and what to do.

Bernard Rimé and his colleagues have found how emotions are implicated in conversation. On about 90% of occasions when people experience an emotion that is salient enough to remember, they discuss it with at least one, and sometimes several other people.[41] Rimé calls this social sharing. He has found it does not decrease the emotion's intensity, as compared with emotions that people had not confided. Nonetheless, people do have an intense drive to share their emotions. They say they receive important benefit from doing so. They say they make sense of their emotions – the places in which reality has breached the surface of their expectations – including the implications of the emotion for themselves and others, as seen both from the inside, and, in terms of the commentary of the friend or relative, from the outside.

Perhaps people talk about their emotions for reasons Collingwood ascribed to artists (discussed in Chapter 2): to make meaningful sense of what they feel. To do this they need to express the emotion in language, the language of conversation. The feeling becomes not just a feeling. It can become consciously understood, and explicitly part of the relationship with the person with whom we are conversing. Conversation is part of our genetically given human adaptation: a part in which we can more reliably attain purposes that are human rather than those of our selfish replicators, our genes. This occurs because in the comparisons of conversation, we explore and define amongst ourselves what it is to be human.

Reading and drama

In Chapter 1 of this book, I started with a poem, and discussed how emotions have preoccupied writers almost from the time writing was invented. In Europe the novel continued the tradition begun by Erasmus and Shakespeare of understanding the emotions that lie beneath the surfaces of social life. Curiously, however, apart from Aristotle's ideas that tragedy induces pity and fear in the audience, and makes for *katharsis* of these emotions, a term perhaps best translated as clearing away obstacles to understanding,[42] the Western tradition of literary theory has not much to say about emotions.

This defect is not shared by an Indian tradition in which literary art had a didactic and spiritual purpose that would enable its readers to live better lives. This tradition is of comparable age to the Greek one. It is thought to have started with Bharata Muni[43] at some time between 400 and 100 BC. Its best surviving sources are about 1,000 years old, from the area that is now Kashmir.[44] In a play, for instance, an actor will enact specific emotions by gesture, tone of voice, and so forth. Then, by an empathetic process, members of the audience experience, or taste, emotions called, in Sanskrit, *rasas*, which correspond to the enacted emotions, but are not exactly the same. They are based on audience members' own experience with what is being portrayed. The Indian theorists postulated nine everyday emotions, and their literary equivalents *rasas* (indicated in brackets):

- delight (the amorous);
- laughter (the comic);
- sorrow (the pitiable or tragic);
- anger (the furious);
- heroism (the heroic);
- fear (the terrible);
- disgust (the odious);
- wonder (the marvelous);
- serenity (the peaceful).

Each well-conceived literary work would concentrate on just one of these, though it would be reached via others, and by what these theorists called transient mental states like discouragement or apprehension. Specific literary emotions, then, correspond to distinct genres: the comic, the tragic, and so forth.

An important difference, within this theory, between everyday emotions and *rasas* was that we are unable properly to understand our emotions in ordinary life because we are made blind by a thick crust of egoism. Because literary emotions could be less imbued with egoism, they allow the reader to see more clearly into their true nature and implications.

Drama and novels are art forms in which we take part in imagination in forms of life that we could never know in our ordinary lives. In them, we develop points of view that Adam Smith thought of as those of sympathetic spectators,[45] taken up in the plans and predicaments of the protagonist, with empathy (or identification, to which it is closely related), and with understanding both of the individual and the social world in which the actions occur. Thus one is able – perhaps in the way that the Indian school believed – to become thoroughly engaged in the emotions of the story, and (in the way the Stoics sought after) compassionate but not egoistically involved, therefore able to understand and evaluate equitably.

Writing

What happens when we do not confide our emotions, do not acknowledge them to ourselves or those whom they might concern? Jamie Pennebaker and his colleagues have suggested that we thereby put ourselves at some risk. In his experiments, participants were asked to come into the laboratory on consecutive days and write for 15 to 30 minutes each day. Some people were asked to write about a superficial topic such as how they used their time. Others were asked to write about an emotionally significant topic, with the following instructions:

> For the next 3 days, I would like for you to write about your very deepest thoughts and feeling about an extremely important emotional issue that has affected you and your life. In your writing I'd like you to really let go and explore your very deepest emotions and thoughts. You might tie your topic to your relationships with others, including parents, lovers, friends, or relatives; to your past, your present, or your future; or to who you have been, who you would like to be, or who you are now. You may write about the same general issues or experiences on all days of writing or on different topics each day. All your writing will be completely confidential. Don't worry about spelling, sentence structure, or grammar. The only rule is that once you begin writing, continue to do so until your time is up.[46]

Many kinds of people have now taken part in the series of experiments of which this is an example, from children to elderly people, and from maximum security prisoners to honors students. People write about a remarkable range of experiences: loves and deaths, incidents of sexual and physical abuse, tragic failures. Many people reported crying and being upset by what they found themselves writing about. They also reported the experience as valuable and meaningful. The consistent results have been that those who wrote about emotionally meaningful experiences underwent substantial lessening in the frequency of their visits to their doctors. That is to say, their general health improved. In some experiments some measures of the immune system's activity were found to start functioning better in those people who wrote about emotionally significant topics, as compared with those who wrote on a bland topic.

Conversation, reading, and writing are not so different. They enable us not just to follow the urges of our emotions, but to think about them in ways that would be much more difficult if we merely kept them to ourselves. As we think about them in such ways, we undertake the education of our emotions, the growth, perhaps, of our emotional intelligence, the construction of an emotional life that is more comprehensible than one of mere urges, a life that is more akin to purposes of the communities in which we live than to those of genetic replicators.

Past and Future

For the ancient Greeks and Romans, the emotions of which one should beware were hubris and anger. We are by no means free of them. In the public domain we still see leaders whose hubris fairly makes one gasp. In the family, nothing seems as destructive as angry abusiveness that is passed on from parents to children: the torch of violence. As Caspi and his colleagues have shown (discussed the in previous chapter), this kind of personal history can interact with the evolutionary history programmed into our genes. In modern times we have become aware of the damage inflicted by other emotional states, most notably depression and anxiety, which, in individualistic societies, disable and restrict huge numbers of people. Depression and the drawn-out versions of fear known as clinical anxiety states have been the principal targets of our modern systems of therapy, both psychological and pharmaceutical.

One psychological movement I discern over the 4,000 years of our civilization's written history is a growing awareness of the limitations of self-interest, a growing consciousness of the other people with whom we share both our more immediate world and the larger world. There has been a growth of respect for others' individuality, and for their rights. In Western psychological studies emotions are more and more being seen not just as states that occur in individual minds and bodies, but as processes that give structure and shape to relationships.[47]

For the future of our human species, I think, it is not so much fear that we have to fear, but the human capacity for contempt: for treating others as outside any human relationship, without concern for their capacity for the emotional life that they share with us.

Notes

PREFACE

1. Stone (1977).
2. Hogan (2003).

CHAPTER 1 MEANING AND AMBIGUITY

1. Lines from Elizabeth Barrett's "Sonnet number 43 'From the Portuguese' (1845-6). There were no Portuguese originals; their title was intended to disguise their autobiographical subject matter.
2. La Rochefoucauld. (1665), Maxim 136.
3. Oatley & Jenkins (1996) offer definitions and fuller discussions of much of the pre-1995 research discussed in this book.
4. James (1884).
5. The term "appraisal" was introduced by Magda Arnold; see Arnold & Gasson (1954).
6. James (1884).
7. Used, for instance, by Francis Bacon.
8. Frijda (1986). On the idea of emotions as conferring urgency, see also Arnold & Gasson (1954) and Tomkins (1970).
9. The conceptual basis of this book is that there are distinct kinds of emotions, each derived from an evolutionary past in which it had a function. James Russell's (2003) alternative view is that emotions are based on a primitive and automatic assessment of positivity and negativity, together with a stronger or weaker arousal.
10. The idea that our emotions occur when our assumed world turns out not to be as we assumed, and reality breaks through, is due to Bernard Rimé (1998).
11. Taine (1882), p. 13, my translation, emphasis in original. See, also, the founding book of modern cognitive psychology: Bartlett (1932).

12. Aubé was the first person, so far as I know, to recognize this importance and to write of emotions in terms of commitments. See, e.g., Aubé & Senteni (1996).
13. The line I have quoted is from p. 170 of the book referenced as Anon (1700 BC), translated from one of the surviving Sumerian stories, "Bilgames (Gilgamesh) and the Bull of Heaven."
14. The "Dispute between a man and his *Ba*," Lichtheim (1973), pp. 163–169, dates from 1990-1785 BC.
15. Rosenberg & Bloom (1990), a reconstruction the original text of first five books of the Bible, by the conjectural writer, J.
16. Hogan (2001).
17. Mencius (c 320 BC), pp. 55–56.
18. Wright (1992), p. 168.
19. See Tetlock (1985).
20. Tetlock (1985), p. 165.
21. Tetlock (1985), p. 166.
22. Tetlock (1985), p. 167.
23. Hogan (2003).
24. Freedman (1978).
25. Oatley & Duncan (1992).
26. Nussbaum (2001).
27. Oatley & Duncan (1992).
28. "The dream of an hour," first published in *Vogue*, 4, 6 Dec. 1894, reprinted Chopin (2000).
29. Chopin (2000), p. 260.
30. Averill & Nunley (1992).
31. Collingwood (1938), pp. 109–110.
32. See, e.g., Oatley (2003)
33. Rousseau (1750).
34. Wordsworth (1802), p. 611.
35. Huizinga (1949), p. 9. See also Rosenwein (2002).
36. Elias (1939).
37. See, e.g., Andreas Capellanus (1185).
38. P.N. Stearns & C.Z. Stearns (1985); Stearns (1999).
39. Reddy (2001).
40. Compare studies of fear and anger following the attack on the World Trade Center of September 11, 2001, by Lerner et al. (2003), and of happiness as an antidote to such fears by Fredrickson et al. (2003).
41. Stone (1977).
42. Patterson et al. (1992).
43. Giddens (1999).

CHAPTER 2 EVOLUTION, CULTURE, AND A NECESSARY AMBIVALENCE

1. Darwin (1859/1871). The utterance by the wife of the Bishop of Worcester is from Leakey & Lewin (1991), p. 16.
2. Dennett (1995).
3. Darwin (1872), p. 40.
4. Darwin (1872).
5. Keltner et al. (2003).
6. Arnold & Gasson (1954).
7. Darwin (1872), p. 225.
8. Cosmides & Tooby (2000).
9. I take 10,000 years ago as the beginning of agriculture and fixed habitations.
10. Wrangham (2001), p. 123.
11. Lee (1984).
12. Tooby & Cosmides (1990); see also Oatley & Johnson-Laird (1987).
13. Oatley & Johnson-Laird (1987).
14. Frijda (1986).
15. Briggs (1970), quotations pp. 282–285.
16. Chagnon (1992), p. xiii.
17. Eibl-Eibesfeldt (1979), p. 117.
18. Chagnon (1992), p. xvi.
19. Ehrenreich (1997); Miller (1993).
20. Shields (2002).
21. Fischer & Manstead (2000).
22. Brody & Hall (2000).
23. Dawkins (1976).
24. Dawkins (1976), p. 234.
25. Dennett (1995) pp. 422–427. The idea of the supertanker robot and robots getting together in pairs, are elaborations of Dennett's idea by Stanovich (2004), pp. 28–32.
26. Stanovich (2004).

CHAPTER 3 MEDICINE FOR THE SOUL

1. Marcus Aurelius (c. 173), p. 45.
2. Marcus Aurelius (c. 173), p. 123.
3. Sorabji (2000), p. 17.
4. Arnold & Gasson (1954), p. 215.
5. *Hamlet*, 2, 2, 245.
6. Nussbaum (1994), p. 103.
7. Donald (1991).

8. Freud (1887–1902), p. 244.
9. Epicurus. (300 BC), p. 651.
10. Nussbaum (1994).
11. Lucretius (c. 55).
12. Nolen-Hoeksema & Jackson (2001).
13. Nussbaum (1994); Jones (1999); Sorabji (2000).
14. Marcus Aurelius (c. 173), p. 47.
15. Sorabji (2000).
16. Stockdale (1995a), p. 4.
17. Epictetus (c. 100), *Discourse I*, p. 13.
18. Stockdale (1995b), p. vii.
19. Stockdale (1995a), p. 9.
20. Sorabji (2000).
21. Sorabji (2000), p. 362.
22. Descartes (1649).
23. Spinoza (1661–75).
24. Spinoza (1661–75), p. 176.
25. Spinoza (1661–75), p. 178.
26. Freud (1905); Oatley (1990).
27. Beck et al. (1979); Hollon et al. (2002).
28. DeRubeis & Crits-Christof (1999).
29. Gross (2002); Butler et al. (2003); Gross & John (2003).
30. Sorabji (2000), p. 169.
31. Konstan (2001), p. 121.
32. Oatley (1997).
33. Popper (1962), p. 270.
34. Hobbes (1651), Chapter 13, p. 96.
35. Cohen (1989).

CHAPTER 4 EMOTIONS AND THE BRAIN

1. Harlow (1868), p. 275.
2. Harlow (1868), p. 277.
3. Harlow (1868), p. 278.
4. H. Damasio et al. (1994)
5. Shallice & Burgess (1991).
6. A. Damasio (1994).
7. Aubé & Senteni (1996).
8. A. Damasio (1994). The error that Damasio attributes to Descartes was to suppose that the soul is different in its substance from the body; it's a bit unfair to Descartes, whose 1649 *Passions of the soul* (which Damasio mentions only in passing) was the founding book of modern neuroscience, and showed how the body works

by sensory systems that detect stimuli, connections via neural mechanisms, and responses of the motor system. Much of it is concerned with the emotions, and shows that though we are moved by them they are also affected by reason (the soul). One could even tease Damasio by suggesting that he makes a version of the error of which he accuses Descartes in that he separates bodily aspects of emotions (Damasio calls them somatic markers) from mental evaluations.

9. Darwin (1872).
10. Freud (1930), p. 257.
11. MacLean (1990, 1993).
12. Cited in Magarshack (1955), p. viii.
13. MacLean (1993) p. 79, emphasis in original.
14. Hughlings-Jackson (1959), p. 58.
15. Aiello & Dunbar (1993).
16. Leick (2001).
17. Jacobs (1970).
18. Donald (1991).
19. Gardner (1993).
20. Braudel (1979).
21. Panksepp (1998, 2001)
22. Parrott (2000).
23. Panksepp (1998), p. 309.
24. Mithen (1996).
25. Lovejoy (1981).
26. Panksepp (1998), p. 15.
27. Collingwood (1938).
28. Descartes (1649)
29. Panksepp (1998), p. 90. In the first part of this book Panksepp gives a useful account of concepts, anatomy, and research methods in brain science.
30. LeDoux (1997).
31. Hart et al. (2000).
32. A. Damasio et al. (2000).
33. Bradwejn (1993).
34. Kramer (1993).
35. Knutson et al. (1998).
36. Double blind trials are essential for testing all drugs with effects on emotions. Double blind means that not only are subjects in the experiment unaware (i.e. blind) to whether they receive the active drug or an inactive placebo, but so are the experimenters who interact with the subjects.
37. Mayberg et al. (1999).

CHAPTER 5 SOCIAL HISTORIES: EMOTIONS AND RELATIONSHIPS

1. This incident of road rage is not untypical. I owe the source to Stanovich (2004). The incident was reported in the *National Post* of November 9, 2001, p. A3, under the headline: "Quebec man kills self in act of road rage." A more extensive discussion may be found in James & Nahl (2000).
2. Oatley & Johnson-Laird (1987, 1996).
3. Lutz (1988).
4. Rozin et al. (2000).
5. Jenkins and two colleagues (Goldberg et al., 1999) argued for the separation of attachment and affection, and Jenkins & Oatley (1996) have discussed the idea of schemas gathering around specific systems of social emotions.
6. Opie & Opie (1951).
7. De Waal (1982), p. 86.
8. The theory that aggression accumulates and is then released when the reservoir containing it overflows was the idea of Konrad Lorenz's famous and influential book of 1967. It has been replaced by the idea of aggression as influenced by social context.
9. Jenkins & Greenbaum (1999), pp. 276–277.
10. Sherif & Sherif (1953).
11. Sherif & Sherif (1953), p. 252.
12. Sherif & Sherif (1953), p. 259.
13. Mesquita (2003); see also Pitt-Rivers (1966); Miller (1993).
14. Fischer & Mosquera (2001).
15. Miller (1994), p. 44.
16. Fromm (1942).
17. Scheff (1997).
18. Braithwaite (1989); Tangney & Dearing (2002).
19. Bowlby (1951), p. 11.
20. Bowlby's original statement, although pointing to important truths, was subsequently shown to be too categorical. See, for instance, Rutter (1972).
21. Kraemer (1992).
22. Goldberg et al. (1999).
23. Darwin (1859/1871), p. 434.
24. Lovejoy (1981); see also Fisher (1992).
25. Konstan (1997).
26. Dunn (2003).
27. Panksepp (1998); K. Lewis (2001).
28. Winnicott (1971).
29. Harris (2000).

30. Fredrickson (1998).
31. Fredrickson (1998).
32. Averill et al. (1998).
33. Etcoff (1999).
34. Orians & Heerwagen (1992).
35. Appleton (1975).
36. Oatley (2003).
37. Shermer (2003).
38. Goodall (1986).
39. Wright (1992).
40. Wright (1992), p. 136.
41. Diamond (1997).
42. Lévi-Strauss (1995), p. 19.
43. Cited in Lévi Strauss (1995), p. 20.
44. Lévi Strauss (1995), p. 20.
45. Raleigh et al. (1991).
46. Keltner (1995); Keltner & Buswell (1997); Keltner & Haidt (1999).
47. Sternberg (2004).
48. Demosthenes (342 BC), p. 87 (19, 65).
49. Konstan (2001), p. 121.
50. Hogan (2001).
51. Zeldin (1994).
52. Menocal (2002)
53. Smith (1759).
54. Hoffman (2000); Eisenberg et al. (2003).
55. Main & George (1985).

CHAPTER 6 INDIVIDUAL HISTORIES

1. Keats (1816–20), p. 288.
2. Jonas (1958).
3. Marvell (1637–78). I thank Joan Peskin for introducing me to this poem.
4. Flanagan (2002).
5. Lord, in Introduction to Marvell (1637–78), p. xxiii.
6. Klibansky et al. (1964)
7. Goldsmith (2003).
8. Caspi et al. (1987, 1988).
9. Harker & Keltner (2001).
10. Costa & McCrae (1996).
11. Freud (1905).
12. Ainsworth et al. (1978).
13. Waters et al. (2000).

14. Schank & Abelson (1977).
15. Tomkins (1979, 1995).
16. James (1890).
17. Jenkins & Oatley (2000).
18. Patterson et al. (1992).
19. Jenkins (2000); Jenkins & Oatley (1996). A similar idea has been described for cultural emotion schemas by Mesquita (2003).
20. Lewis & Douglas (1998); Lewis & Granic (2000).
21. Magai & Haviland-Jones (2002).
22. Shostrom (1966).
23. Keltner et al. (2003).
24. C. R. Rogers (1972).
25. H. E. Rogers (1965).
26. Magai & Haviland-Jones (2002), p. 57.
27. Magai & Haviland-Jones (2002), p. 57.
28. Magai & Haviland-Jones (2002), p. 50.
29. Magai & Haviland-Jones (2002), p. 88.
30. Magai & Haviland-Jones (2002), p. 90; next quote p. 89.
31. Proust (1913–27). II, p. 565, I owe this quotation to Goldie (2000).
32. Magai & Haviland-Jones (2002), p. 57.
33. Waters et al. (2000).
34. Weinfield et al. (2000).
35. Augustine (401).
36. James (1902); Oatley & Djikic (2002).
37. James (1902), pp. 195 and 198.
38. Quinton et al. (1984); Quinton & Rutter (1988).
39. Fleming et al. (2002).

CHAPTER 7 EMOTIONAL DISORDERS

1. Lloyd (1978), p. 134.
2. Burton (1621).
3. Kessler (2002).
4. Brown & Harris (1978). For a briefer account of depression in relation to life events, see Oatley & Bolton (1985).
5. This case of Mrs Trent (not her real name) is paraphrased from Brown & Harris (1978), pp. 28–29.
6. American Psychiatric Association (1994).
7. These figures, i.e. 21 percent of women suffering an episode of major depression at some time in their lives, or of 9 percent of women with chronic depression during a year, are known, respectively, as lifetime prevalence and one-year prevalence. Brown and Harris's principal results were not on prevalence, however, but on incidence: the

number of new onsets of depression during a year; in this case 8 percent of the women interviewed.

8. A breakdown in this sense is called a non-psychotic psychiatric breakdown. Breakdowns that involve psychosis, such as with schizophrenia or a manic episode, do occur, but they are rarer, are more closely dependent on genetic factors, and have a different relation to life events.
9. Kendler et al. (2003).
10. Plomin & Bergeman (1991).
11. Kendler et al. (2001).
12. Shorter (1997).
13. Kraepelin (1899).
14. Kendler & Prescott (1999); Kendler (2001).
15. American Psychiatric Association (1994).
16. Freud (1905).
17. Snow (1855); Longmate (1966).
18. Jenkins (2000); Caspi et al. (1987).
19. Watson & Crick (1953).
20. Caspi et al. (2003).
21. Oatley & Perring (1991).
22. See, e.g., Webster (1995).
23. Patterson et al. (1992).
24. Caspi et al.(2002).

CHAPTER 8 EMOTIONAL INTELLIGENCE

1. I mean either the noun "intelligence" or the adjective "intelligent."
2. Wordsworth (1802) is among the earliest literary figures to write the term "emotion" in the modern sense in English. See also Dixon (2001).
3. Salovey (2003). Their original article was Salovey & Mayer (1990). An extract is reprinted in Jenkins et al. (1998), pp. 313–319.
4. Salovey et al. (in press).
5. Mathews et al. (2002).
6. Field (1934).
7. Field (1934) quotes in this paragraph are from, respectively, pp. 36 and 28.
8. Field (1934), p. 26.
9. Field (1934), p. 85.
10. Field (1934), p. 115.
11. Field (1934). This and the next quotation are from p. 193.
12. Keltner et al. (2003).
13. Ekman & O'Sullivan (1991).

14. Ekman (2003).
15. Adolphs et al. (1994).
16. Planalp et al. (1996).
17. Isen et al. (1987).
18. Baron (1987).
19. Seligman (2002).
20. Erasmus (1508), p. 106.
21. Quotations from Erasmus's Adages are scattered through Shakespeare's plays. When Hamlet asks himself whether "to take arms against a sea of troubles" (*Hamlet* 3, 1, 61), the phrase "sea of troubles" is from this source.
22. See, for instance, Carol Reed's 1949 film *The third man*, which, amongst other things, offers the very Shakespearean juxtaposition of Harry Lime's racketeering with the sewers of Vienna.
23. *Hamlet* 5, 2, 78–79.
24. *Hamlet* 5, 2, 160.
25. Spinoza (1661–75), p. 194.
26. Gombrich (1972), pp. 41–42.
27. Cited in Gombrich (1972), p. 41.
28. Cited in Gombrich (1972), p. 42.
29. Jenkins et al. (1998), p. 315.
30. Csikszentmihalyi (1990).
31. Csikszentmihalyi (1990), pp. 39–40.
32. Csikszentmihalyi (1990). The first quotation in this paragraph is from p. 55, the other two are from p. 53.
33. See also Seligman (2002).
34. Salovey et al. (2004).
35. Lopes et al. (in press).
36. Dunbar (1996).
37. Fussell (2002).
38. Dunbar (2003).
39. Dunbar (in press).
40. Zeldin (1998), p. 7.
41. Rimé et al. (1998).
42. Nussbaum (1986).
43. Bharata Muni (200 BC).
44. Ingalls et al. (1990).
45. Nussbaum (1995).
46. Pennebaker (1997), p. 162. See also Pennebaker et al. (2001); Niederhoffer & Pennebaker (2002).
47. See, e.g., Parkinson et al. (2004).

References

Adolphs, R., Tranel, D., Damasio, H., & Damasio, A. (1994). Impaired recognition of emotion in facial expressions following bilateral damage to the human amygdala. *Nature, 372,* 669–672.

Aiello, L. C., & Dunbar, R. I. M. (1993). Neocortex size, group size, and the evolution of language. *Current Anthropology, 34,* 184–193.

Ainsworth, M. D. S., Blehar, M. C., Walters, E., & Wall, S. (1978). *Patterns of attachment: A psychological study of the strange situation.* Hillsdale, NJ: Erlbaum.

American Psychiatric Association. (1994). *Diagnostic and statistical manual of mental disorders* (4th edition: *DSM-IV*). Washington, DC: American Psychiatric Association.

Andreas Capellanus. (1185). *The art of courtly love* (J.J. Parry, Trans.). New York: Columbia University Press (current edition 1960).

Anon. (1700 BC). *The epic of Gilgamesh: The Babylonian epic poem and other texts in Akkadian and Sumerian* (A. George, Trans.). London: Penguin (current edition 2000).

Appleton, J. (1975). *The experience of landscape.* Chichester: Wiley.

Arnold, M. B., & Gasson, J. A. (1954). Feelings and emotions as dynamic factors in personality integration. In M. B. Arnold & J. A. Gasson (Eds.), *The human person* (pp. 294–313). New York: Ronald. Reprinted in M. B. Arnold (Ed.) (1968) *The nature of emotion* (pp. 203–221). Harmondsworth: Penguin.

Aubé, M., & Senteni, A. (1996). Emotions as committments operators: A foundation for control structure in multi-agents systems. In W. Van de Velde & J. W. Perram (Eds.), *Agents breaking away: Proceedings of the 7th European Workshop on MAAMAW, Lecture notes on artificial intelligence, No. 1038* (pp. 13–25). Berlin: Springer.

Augustine. (401). *The confessions* (M. Boulding, Trans.). New York: Vintage (currrent edition 1998).

Averill, J. , & Nunley, E. (1992). *Voyages of the heart: Living an emotionally creative life.* New York: Free Press.

Averill, J., Stanat, P., & More, T. (1998). Aesthetics and environment. *Review of General Psychology, 2,* 153–174.

Baron, R. A. (1987). Interviewer's mood and reaction to job applicants. *Journal of Applied Social Psychology, 17,* 911–926.

Barrett Browning, E. (1845–6). Sonnets from the Portuguese. In *Selected poems* (C. Graham, Ed., p. 231). London: Dent Everyman (current edition 1996).

Bartlett, F. C. (1932). *Remembering: A study in experimental and social psychology.* Cambridge: Cambridge University Press.

Beck, A. T., Rush, A. J., Shaw, B. F., & Emery, G. (1979). *Cognitive therapy of depression.* New York: Guilford.

Bharata Muni. (200 BC). *Natyasastra.* Bangalore: IBH Prakashana (current edition 1986).

Bowlby, J. (1951). *Child care and the growth of love.* Harmondsworth: Penguin.

Bradwejn, J. (1993). Neurobiological investigations into the role of cholecystokinin in panic disorder. *Journal of Psychiatry and Neuroscience, 18,* 178–188.

Braithwaite, J. (1989). *Crime, shame and reintegration.* Cambridge: Cambridge University Press.

Braudel, F. (1979). *Civilization and capitalism, 15th to 18th Century, Vol. 1. The structures of everyday life: The limits of the possible* (M. Kochan & S. Reynolds, Trans.). London: Fontana (current edition 1985).

Briggs, J. L. (1970). *Never in anger: Portrait of an Eskimo family.* Cambridge, MA: Harvard University Press.

Brody, L. R., & Hall, J. A. (2000). Gender, emotion, and expression. In M. Lewis & J. Haviland-Jones (Eds.), *Handbook of emotions* (2nd edition, pp. 338–349). New York: Guilford.

Brown, G. W., & Harris, T. O. (1978). *Social origins of depression: A study of psychiatric disorder in women.* London: Tavistock.

Burton, R. (1621). *The anatomy of melancholy: What it is, with all the kinds, causes, symptomes, prognostickes & several cures of it.* London: Dent (current edition 1932).

Butler, E. A., Egloff, B., Wilhelm, F. H., Smith, N. C., Erickson, E. A., & Gross, J. J. (2003). The social consequences of expressive suppression. *Emotion, 3,* 48–67.

Caspi, A., Elder, G. H., & Bem, D. J. (1987). Moving against the world: Life course patterns of explosive children. *Developmental Psychology, 23,* 308–313.

Caspi, A., Elder, G. H., & Bem, D. J. (1988). Moving away from the world: Life-course patterns of shy children. *Developmental Psychology, 24,* 824–831.

Caspi, A., McClay, J., Moffitt, T. E., Mill, J., Martin, J., Craig, I. W., Taylor, A., & Poulton, R. (2002). Role of genotype in the cycle of violence in maltreated children. *Science, 297,* 851–854.

Caspi, A., Sugden, K., Moffitt, T. E., Taylor, A., Craig, I. W., Taylor, A., Harrington, H., McClay, J., Mill, J., Martin, J., Braithwaite, A., & Poulton, R. (2003). Influence on life stress on depression: Moderation by a polymorphism in the 5-HTT gene. *Science, 301,* 386–389

Chagnon, N., A. (1992). *Yanomamö: The last days of Eden.* New York: Harcourt Brace Jovanovich

Chopin, K. (2000). *The awakening and other stories* (P. Knights, Ed.). Oxford: Oxford University Press.

Cohen, M. N. (1989). *Health and the rise of civilization.* New Haven, CT: Yale University Press.

Collingwood, R. G. (1938). *The principles of art.* Oxford: Oxford University Press.

Cosmides, L., & Tooby, J. (2000). Evolutionary psychology and the emotions. In M. Lewis & J. Haviland-Jones (Eds.), *Handbook of emotions* (2nd edition, pp. 91–115). New York: Guilford.

Costa, P. T., & McCrae, R. R. (1996). Mood and personality in adulthood. In C. Magai & S. H. McFadden (Eds.), *Handbook of emotion, adult development, and aging* (pp. 369–383). San Diego: Academic Press.

Csikszentmihalyi, M. (1990). *Flow: The psychololgy of optimal experience.* New York: HarperCollins.

Damasio, A. (1994). *Descartes' error.* New York: Putnam.

Damasio, A., Grabowski, T. J., Bechara, A., Hanna, D., Ponto, L. L. B., Parvizi, J., & Hichwa, R. D. (2000). Sub-cortical and cortical brain activity during the feeling of self-generated emotions. *Nature Neuroscience, 3,* 1049–1056.

Damasio, H., Grabowski, T. J., Frank, R., Galaburda, A.M., & Damasio, A. (1994). The return of Phineas Gage: The skull of a famous patient yields clues about the brain. *Science, 264,* 1102–1105.

Darwin, C. (1859/1871). *The origin of species by means of natural selection/ The descent of man and selection in relation to sex.* New York: Modern Library (current edition undated).

Darwin, C. (1872). *The expression of the emotions in man and animals* (2nd edition of 1889). London: Murray.

Dawkins, R. (1976). *The selfish gene.* Oxford: Oxford University Press.

Demosthenes. (342 BC). *On the false embassy* (Oration 19) (D. M. MacDowell, Ed. and Trans.). Oxford: Oxford University Press (current edition 2000).

Dennett, D. (1995). *Darwin's dangerous idea: Evolution and the meaning of life.* New York: Simon & Schuster.

DeRubeis, R. J., & Crits-Christof, P. (1999). Empirically supported individual and group psychological treatments for adult mental disorders. *Journal of Consulting and Clinical Psychology, 66,* 37–52.

Descartes, R. (1649). *Passions of the soul*. In E. L. Haldane & G. R. Ross (Eds.), *The philosophical works of Descartes*. New York: Dover (current edition 1911).

de Waal, F. (1982). *Chimpanzee politics*. New York: Harper & Row.

Diamond, J. (1997). *Guns, germs, and steel: The fates of human societies*. New York: Norton.

Dixon, T. (2001). The psychology of the emotions in Britain and America in the nineteenth century: The role of religious and anti-religious commitments. *Osiris*, *16*, 288–320.

Donald, M. (1991). *Origins of the modern mind*. Cambridge, MA: Harvard University Press.

Dunbar, R. I. M. (1996). *Grooming, gossip and the evolution of language*. London: Faber & Faber.

Dunbar, R. I. M. (2003). The social brain: Mind, language, and society in evolutionary perspective. *Annual Review of Anthropology*, *32*, 163–181.

Dunbar, R. I. M. (in press). Language, music, and laughter in evolutionary perspective.

Dunn, J. (2003). Emotional development in early childhood: A social relationship perspective. In R. J. Davidson, K. R. Scherer, & H. H. Goldsmith (Eds.), *Handbook of affective sciences* (pp. 332–346). New York: Oxford University Press.

Ehrenreich, B. (1997). *Blood rites: Origins and history of the passions of war*. New York: Holt.

Eibl-Eibesfeldt, I. (1979). *The biology of peace and war* (E. Mosbacher, Trans.). New York: Viking.

Eisenberg, N., Losoya, S., & Spinrad, T. (2003). Affect and prosocial responding. In R. J. Davidson, K. R. Scherer, & H. H. Goldsmith (Eds.), *Handbook of affective sciences* (pp. 787–803). New York: Oxford University Press.

Ekman, P. (2003) *Emotions revealed: Recognizing faces and feelings to improve communication*. New York: Holt.

Ekman, P., & O'Sullivan, M. (1991). Who can catch a liar? *American Psychologist*, *46*, 913–920.

Elias, N. (1939). *The civilizing process, The history of manners* (E. Jephcott, Trans.). New York: Urizen Books (current edition 1978).

Epictetus. (c. 100). *Discourses and Encheiridion* (W. A. Oldfather, Trans.). Cambridge, MA: Loeb–Harvard University Press (current edition 1925).

Epicurus. (300 BC). Epicurus: Letter to Menoeceus. In R. D. Hicks (Ed.), *Diogenes Laertius: Lives of the eminent philosophers* (Vol. 2, Book 10, pp. 528–677). Cambridge, MA: Loeb Classical Library, Harvard University Press (current edition 1931).

Erasmus, D. (1508). *Praise of folly* (R.M. Adams, Ed. & Trans.). New York: Norton (current edition 1989).

Etcoff, N. L. (1999). *The survival of the prettiest: The science of beauty*. New York: Doubleday.

Field, J. (1934). *A life of one's own*. Harmondsworth: Penguin (current edition 1952).

Fischer, A. H., & Manstead, A. S. R. (2000). The relation between gender and emotions in different cultures. In A. H. Fischer (Ed.), *Gender and emotion: Social psychological perspectives* (pp. 71–93). Cambridge: Cambridge University Press.

Fischer, A. H., & Mosquera, P. M. R. (2001). What concerns men? Women or other men? A critical appraisal of the evolutionary theory of sex differences in aggression. *Psychology, Evolution & Gender, 3*, 5–25.

Fisher, H. E. (1992). *Anatomy of love*. New York: Norton.

Flanagan, O. (2002). *The problem of the soul: Two visions of mind and how to reconcile them*. New York: Basic Books.

Fleming, A. S., Kraemer, G. W., Gonzalez, A., Lovie, V., Rees, S., & Melo, A. (2002). Mothering begets mothering: The transmission of behavior and its neurobiology across generations. *Pharmacology, Biochemistry and Behavior, 73*, 61–75.

Fredrickson, B. L. (1998). What good are positive emotions? *Review of General Psychology, 2*, 1–20.

Fredrickson, B. L., Tugade, M. M., Waugh, C. E., & Larkin, G. R. (2003). What good are positive emotions in crises? A prospective study of resilience and emotions following the terrorist attacks on the United States on September 11th 2001. *Journal of Personality & Social Psychology, 84*, 365–376.

Freedman, J. L. (1978). *Happy people: What happiness is, who has it and why*. New York: Harcourt Brace Jovanovich.

Freud, S. (1887–1902). *The origins of psychoanalysis: Letters to Wilhelm Fliess 1887–1902* (M. Bonaparte, A. Freud, & E. Kris, Eds.). New York: Basic Books (current edition 1954).

Freud, S. (1905). Fragment of an analysis of a case of hysteria (Dora). In J. Strachey & A. Richards (Eds.), *The Pelican Freud Library, Vol. 8: Case histories, II* (pp. 29–164). London: Penguin (current edition 1979).

Freud, S. (1930). Civilization and its discontents. In A. Dickson (Ed.), *The Pelican Freud Library, Vol. 12: Civilization, society and religion* (pp. 243–340). London: Penguin (current edition 1984).

Frijda, N. H. (1986). *The emotions*. Cambridge: Cambridge University Press.

Fromm, E. (1942). *Fear of freedom*. London: Routledge & Kegan Paul (current edition 1960).

Fussell, S.R. (2002) *The verbal communication of emotions: Interdisciplinary perspectives*. Mahwah, NJ: Erlbaum.

Gardner, H. (1993). *Creating minds: An anatomy of creativity seen through the lives of Freud, Einstein, Picasso, Stravinsky, Eliot, Graham, and Ghandi*. New York: Basic Books.

Giddens, A. (1999). *BBC Reith Lectures: Runaway World: Lecture 4: Family.* www.lse.ac.uk/Giddens/reith_99/week4/week4.htm.

Goldberg, S., Grusec, J. E., & Jenkins, J. M. (1999). Confidence in protection: Arguments for a narrow definition of attachment. *Journal of Family Psychology, 13,* 475–483.

Goldie, P. (2000). *The emotions: A philosophical exploration.* Oxford: Oxford University Press.

Goldsmith, H. H. (2003). Genetics of emotional development. In R. J. Davidson, K. R. Scherer, & H. H. Goldsmith (Eds.), *Handbook of affective sciences* (pp. 295–319). New York: Oxford University Press.

Goleman, D. (1995). *Emotional intelligence.* New York: Bantam.

Gombrich, E. (1972). Botticelli's mythologies: A study in the neo-Platonic symbolism of his circle. In E. H. Gombrich (Ed.), *Symbolic images: Studies in the art of the Renaissance* (pp. 31–81). London: Phaidon.

Goodall, J. (1986). *The chimpanzees of Gombe: Patterns of behavior.* Cambridge, MA: Harvard University Press.

Gross, J. J. (2002). Emotion regulation: Affective, cognitive, and social consequences. *Psychophysiology, 39,* 281–291

Gross, J. J., & John, O. P. (2003). Individual differences in two emotion regulation processes: Implications for affect, relationships, and well-being. *Journal of Personality & Social Psychology, 85,* 348–362.

Harker, L., & Keltner, D. (2001). Expression of positive emotion in women's college yearbook pictures and their relationship to personality and life outcomes across adulthood. *Journal of Personality & Social Psychology, 80,* 112–124.

Harlow, J.M. (1868). Recovery from the passage of an iron bar through the head. Reprinted in *History of Psychiatry, 4* (1993), 274–281.

Harris, P. L. (2000). *The work of the imagination.* Oxford: Blackwell.

Hart, A. J., Whalen, P. J., Shin, L. M., McInerney, S. C., Fischer, H., & Rauch, S. (2000). Differential response of the human amygdala to racial outgroup vs. ingroup face stimuli. *Neuroreport, 11,* 2351–2354.

Hobbes, T. (1651). *Leviathan.* Toronto: Broadview (current edition 2002).

Hoffman, M. L. (2000). *Empathy and moral development: Implications for caring and justice.* New York: Cambridge University Press.

Hogan, P. C. (2001). The epilogue of suffering: Heroism, empathy, ethics. *SubStance, 94/95,* 119–143.

Hogan, P. C. (2003). *The mind and its stories.* Cambridge: Cambridge University Press.

Hollon, S. D., Haman, K. L., & Brown, L. L. (2002). Cognitive-behavioral treatment of depression. In I. H. Gotlib & C. L. Hammen (Eds.), *Handbook of depression* (pp. 383–403). New York: Guilford.

Hughlings-Jackson, J. (1959). *Selected writings of John Hughlings-Jackson, Vol. 2* (J. Taylor, Ed.). New York: Basic Books.

Huizinga, J. (1949). *The waning of the Middle Ages: A study of the forms of life, thought and art in France and the Netherlands in the dawn of the Renaissance.* New York: Doubleday.

Ingalls, D. H. H., Masson, J. M., & Patwardhan, M. V. (1990). *The Dhvanyaloka of Anandavardana with the Locana of Abhinavagupta.* Cambridge, MA: Harvard University Press.

Isen, A. M., Daubman, K. A., & Nowicki, G. P. (1987). Positive affect facilitates creative problem solving. *Journal of Personality and Social Psychology, 52,* 1122–1131.

Jacobs, J. (1970). *The economy of cities.* New York: Vintage.

James, L., & Nahl, D. (2000). *Road rage and aggressive driving: Steeriing clear of highway warfare.* Amherst, NY: Prometheus Books.

James, W. (1884). What is an emotion? *Mind, 9,* 188–205.

James, W. (1890). *The principles of psychology.* New York: Dover (current edition 1950).

James, W. (1902). *The varieties of religious experience.* New York: Longmans, Green, & Co.

Jenkins, J. M. (2000) Marital conflict and children's emotions: The development of an anger organization. *Journal of Marriage and the Family, 62,* 723–736.

Jenkins, J. M., & Greenbaum, R. (1999). Intention and emotion in child psychopathology: Building cooperative plans. In P. D. Zelazo, J. W. Astington, & D. R. Olson (Eds.), *Developing theories of intention: Social understanding and self-control* (pp. 269–291). Mahwah, NJ: Erlbaum.

Jenkins, J. M., & Oatley, K. (1996). The development of emotion schemas in children: The processes underlying psychopathology. In W. F. Flack & J. D. Laird (Eds.), *Emotions and psychopathology* (pp. 45–56). New York: Oxford University Press.

Jenkins, J. M., & Oatley, K. (2000). Psychopathology and short-term emotion: The balance of affects. *Journal of Child Psychology and Psychiatry, 41,* 463–472.

Jenkins, J. M., Oatley, K., & Stein, N.L. (Eds.). (1998). *Human emotions: A reader.* Oxford: Blackwell.

Jonas, H. (1958). *The gnostic religion: The message of the alien God and the beginnings of Christianity.* Boston: Beacon.

Jones, P. (1999). *An intelligent person's guide to the classics.* London: Duckworth.

Keats, J. (1816–20). *Selected poems and letter of Keats* (D. Bush, Ed.). New York: Houghton Mifflin (current edition 1959).

Keltner, D. (1995). Signs of appeasement: Evidence for the distinct displays of embarrassment, amusement, and shame. *Journal of Personality and Social Psychology, 68,* 441–454.

Keltner, D., & Buswell, B. N. (1997). Embarrassment: Its distinct forms and appeasement functions. *Psychological Bulletin, 122,* 250–270.

Keltner, D., & Haidt, J. (1999). Social functions of emotions at four levels of analysis. *Cognition and Emotion, 13,* 505–521.

Keltner, D., Ekman, P., Gonzaga, G. C., & Beer, J. (2003). Facial expression of emotion. In R. J. Davidson, K. R. Scherer, & H. H. Goldsmith (Eds.), *Handbook of affective sciences* (pp. 415–432). New York: Oxford University Press.

Kendler, K. S. (2001). Twin studies of psychiatric illness: An update. *Archives of General Psychiatry, 58,* 1005–1014.

Kendler, K. S., & Prescott, C. A. (1999). A population-based twin study of lifetime major depression in men and women. *Archives of General Psychiatry, 56,* 39–44.

Kendler, K. S., Thornton, L. M., & Gardner, C. O. (2001). Genetic risk, number of previous episodes, and stressful life events in predicting onset of major depression. *American Journal of Psychiatry, 158,* 582–586.

Kendler, K. S., Hettema, J. M., Butera, F., Garnder, C. O., & Prescott, C. A. (2003). Life event dimemsions of loss, humiliation, entrapment, and danger. *Archives of General Psychiatry, 60,* 789–796.

Kessler, R. C. (2002). Epidemiology of depression. In I. H. Gotlib & C. L. Hammen (Eds.), *Handbook of depression* (pp. 23–42). New York: Guilford.

Kessler, R. C., McGonagle, K. A., Zhao, S., Nelson, C. P., Hughes, M., Eshleman, S., Wittchen, H.-U., & Kendler, K. S. (1994). Lifetime and 12-month prevalence of *DSM-III-R* psychiatric disorders in the United States: Results from the National Comorbidity Survey. *Archives of General Psychiatry, 51,* 8–19

Klibansky, R., Panofsky, E., & Saxl, F. (1964). *Saturn and melancholy.* London: Nelson.

Knutson, B., Wolkowitz, O. M., Cole, S. W., Chan, T., Moore, E. A., Johnson, R. C., Terpstra, J., Turner, R. A., & Reus, V. I. (1998). Selective alteration of personality and social behavior by serotonergic intervention. *American Journal of Psychiatry, 155,* 373–379.

Konstan, D. (1997). *Friendship in the classical world.* Cambridge: Cambridge University Press.

Konstan, D. (2001). *Pity transformed.* London: Duckworth.

Kraemer, G. W. (1992). A psychobiological theory of attachment. *Behavioral and Brain Sciences, 15,* 493–541.

Kraepelin, E. (1899). *Psychiatrie: Ein Lehrbuch für Studirende und Aerzte* (6th edition). Leipzig: Barth.

Kramer, P. D. (1993). *Listening to Prozac.* New York: Viking.

La Rochefoucauld. (1665). *Maxims* (L. Tancock, Trans.). Harmondsworth: Penguin (current edition 1959).

Leakey, R., & Lewin, R. (1991). *Origins.* London: Penguin.

LeDoux, J. (1997). *The emotional brain: The mysterious underpinnings of emotional life.* New York: Simon & Schuster.

Lee, R. B. (1984). *The Dobe !Kung*. New York: Holt, Rinehart & Winston.

Leick, G. (2001). *The invention of the city*. London: Penguin.

Lerner, J. S., Gonzalez, R. M., Small, D. A., & Fischhoff, B. (2003). Effects of fear and anger on perceived risks of terrorism: A national field experiment. *Psychological Science, 14*, 144–150.

Lévi-Strauss, C. (1995). Saudades do Brasil. *New York Review of Books*, December, 19–27.

Lewis, K. (2001). A comparative study of primate play behavior: Implications for the study of cognition. *Folia Primatatologica, 71*, 417–421.

Lewis, M. D., & Douglas, L. (1998). A dynamic systems approach to cognition–emotion interactions in development. In M. F. Masculo & S. Griffin (Eds.), *What develops in emotional development?* (pp. 159–188). New York: Plenum.

Lewis, M. D., & Granic, I. (Eds.). (2000). *Emotion, development, and self-organization: Dynamic systems approaches to emotional development*. New York: Cambridge University Press.

Lichtheim, M. (1973). *Ancient Egyptian literature, Vol. 1: The Old and Middle Kingdoms*. Berkeley: University of California Press.

Lloyd, G. E. R. (Ed.). (1978). *Hippocratic writings*. Harmondsworth: Penguin.

Longmate, N. (1966). *King cholera: The biography of a disease*. London: Hamish Hamilton.

Lopes, P. N., Salovey, P., & Strauss, R. (2003). Emotional intelligence, personality, and the perceived quality of social relationships. *Personality and Individual Differences, 35*, 641–658.

Lopes, P. N., Nezlek, J. B., Schütz, A., Sellin, I., & Salovey, P. (in press). Emotional intelligence and social interaction. *Personality and Social Psychology Bulletin*.

Lorenz, K. (1967). *On aggression* (M. Latzke, Trans.). London: Methuen.

Lovejoy, C. O. (1981). The origin of man. *Science, 211*, 341–350.

Lucretius. (c. 55). *On the nature of things* (A. M. Esolen, Ed. & Trans.). Baltimore, MD: Johns Hopkins University Press (current edition 1995).

Lutz, C. A. (1988). *Unnatural emotions: Everyday sentiments on a Micronesian atoll and their challenge to Western theory*. Chicago: University of Chicago Press.

MacLean, P. D. (1990). *The triune brain in evolution*. Plenum: New York.

MacLean, P. D. (1993). Cerebral evolution of emotion. In M. Lewis & J. M. Haviland (Eds.), *Handbook of emotions* (pp. 67–83). New York: Guilford.

Magai, C., & Haviland-Jones, J. (2002). *The hidden genius of emotion: Life span transformations of personality*. New York: Cambridge University Press.

Magarshack, D. (1955). Introduction to F. Dostoevsky, *The idiot* (pp. vii–xxv). Harmondsworth: Penguin.

Main, M., & George, C. (1985). Response of abused and disadvantaged toddlers to distress in playmates: A study in the daycare setting. *Developmental Psychology, 21*, 407–412.

Marcus Aurelius. (c. 173). *Meditations* (M. Staniforth, Trans.). London: Penguin.

Marvell, A. (1637–78). *Complete poetry* (G. de F. Lord, Ed.). New York: Modern Library, Random House (current edition 1968).

Matthews, G., Zeidner, M., & Roberts, R. (2002). *Emotional intelligence: Science and myth*. Cambridge, MA: MIT Press.

Mayberg, H. S., Liotti, M., Brannan, S. K., McGinnis, S., Maharin, R. K., Jerabek, P. A., Silva, J. A., Tekell, J. L., Martin, C. C., Lancaster, J. L., & Fox, P. T. (1999). Reciprocal limbic cortical function and negative mood: Converging PET findings in depression and normal sadness. *American Journal of Psychiatry, 156*, 675–682.

Mencius. (c 320 BC). *Mencius* (D. C. Lau, Trans.). London: Penguin (current edition 1970).

Menocal, M. R. (2002). *The ornament of the world: How Muslims, Jews, and Christians created a culture of tolerance in medieval Spain*. Boston: Little Brown.

Mesquita, B. (2003). Emotions as dynamic cultural phenomena. In R. J. Davidson, K. R. Scherer, & H. H. Goldsmith (Eds.), *Handbook of affective sciences* (pp. 871–890). New York: Oxford University Press.

Miller, W. I. (1993). *Humiliation: And other essays on honor, social discomfort and violence*. Ithaca, NY: Cornell University Press.

Miller, W. I. (1994). The politics of emotion display in heroic society. Paper presented at the Proceedings of the VIIIth conference of the International Society for Research on Emotions, Cambridge.

Mithen, S. (1996). *The prehistory of the mind: The cognitive origins of art and science*. London: Thames and Hudson.

Niederhoffer, K. G., & Pennebaker, J. W. (2002). Sharing one's story: On the benefits of writing or talking about emotional experience. In C. R. Snyder & S. J. Lopez (Eds.), *Handbook of positive psychology* (pp. 573–583). New York: Oxford University Press.

Nolen-Hoeksema, S., & Jackson, B. (2001). Mediators of gender differences in rumination. *Psychology of Women Quarterly, 25*, 37–47.

Nussbaum, M. C. (1986). *The fragility of goodness: Luck and ethics in Greek tragedy and philosophy*. Cambridge: Cambridge University Press.

Nussbaum, M. C. (1994). *The therapy of desire: Theory and practice in Hellenistic ethics*. Princeton, NJ: Princeton University Press.

Nussbaum, M. C. (1995). *Poetic justice: The literary imagination and public life*. Boston: Beacon.

Nussbaum, M. C. (2001). *Upheavals of thought: The intelligence of emotions*. New York: Cambridge University Press.

Oatley, K. (1990). Freud's psychology of intention: The case of Dora. *Mind and Language, 5,* 69–86.

Oatley, K. (1997). Emotions and human flourishing (extended review of Martha Nussbaum's *Therapy of desire,* and *Poetic justice*). *Cognition and Emotion, 11,* 307–330.

Oatley, K. (2003). Creative expression and communication of emotion in the visual and narrative arts. In R. J. Davidson, K. R. Scherer, & H. H. Goldsmith (Eds.), *Handbook of affective sciences* (pp. 481–502). New York: Oxford University Press.

Oatley, K., & Bolton, W. (1985). A social-cognitive theory of depression in reaction to life events. *Psychological Review, 92,* 372–388.

Oatley, K., & Djikic, M. (2002). Emotions and transformation: Varieties of experience of identity. *Journal of Consciousness Studies, 9–10,* 97–116,

Oatley, K., & Duncan, E. (1992). Incidents of emotion in daily life. In K. T. Strongman (Ed.), *International review of studies on emotion* (Vol. 2, pp. 250–293). Chichester: Wiley.

Oatley, K., & Jenkins, J. M. (1996). *Understanding emotions.* Oxford: Blackwell.

Oatley, K., & Johnson-Laird, P. N. (1987). Towards a cognitive theory of emotions. *Cognition and Emotion, 1,* 29–50.

Oatley, K., & Johnson-Laird, P. N. (1996). The communicative theory of emotions: Empirical tests, mental models, and implications for social interaction. In L. L. Martin & A. Tesser (Eds.), *Striving and feeling: Interactions among goals, affect, and self-regulation* (pp. 363–393). Mahwah, NJ: Erlbaum.

Oatley, K., & Perring, C. (1991). A longitudinal study of psychological and social factors affecting recovery from psychiatric breakdown. *British Journal of Psychiatry, 158,* 28–32.

Opie, I., & Opie, P. (1951). *The Oxford dictionary of nursery rhymes.* Oxford: Oxford University Press.

Orians, G. H., & Heerwagen, J. H. (1992). Evolved responses to landscapes. In J. H. Barkow, L. Cosmides, & J. Tooby (Eds.), *The adapted mind* (pp. 555–579). New York: Oxford University Press.

Panksepp, J. (1998). *Affective neuroscience: The foundations of human and animal emotions.* Oxford: Oxford University Press.

Panksepp, J. (2001). The neuro-evolutionary cusp between emotions and cognitions: Implications for understanding consciousness and the emergence of a unified mind science. *Evolution and Cognition, 7,* 141–163.

Parkinson, B., Fischer, A. H., & Manstead, A. S. R. (2004). *Emotion in social relations: Cultural, group, and interpersonal processes.* Philadelphia, PA: Psychology Press.

Parrott, W. G. (2000). My emotions and Ur-emotions. Paper presented at the International Society for Research on Emotions, Quebec City.

Pascal, B. (1670). *Pensées and other writings* (H. Levi, Trans.). Oxford: Oxford University Press (current edition 1995).

Patterson, G. R., Reid, J. B., & Dishion, T. J. (1992). *Anti-social boys*. Eugene, OR: Castalia.

Pennebaker, J.W. (1997). Writing about emotional experiences as a therapeutic process. *Psychological Science, 8,* 162–166,

Pennebaker, J. W., Zech, E., & Rimé, B. (2001). Disclosing and sharing emotion: psychological, social, and health consequences. In M. S. Stroebe, R. O. Hansson, W. Stroebe, & H. Schut (Eds.), *Handbook of bereavement research: Consequences, coping, and care* (pp. 517–543). Washington, DC: American Psychological Association.

Pitt-Rivers, J. (1966). Honor and social status. In J. G. Peristany (Ed.), *Honor and shame: The values of Mediterranean society* (pp. 19–78). Chicago: University of Chicago Press.

Planalp, S., DeFrancisco, V. L., & Rutherford, D. (1996). Varieties of cues to emotion. *Cognition and Emotion, 10,* 137–153.

Plomin, R., & Bergeman, C. S. (1991). The nature of nurture: Genetic influence on environmental measures. *Behvioral and Brain Sciences, 14,* 373–427.

Popper, K. R. (1962). *The open society and its enemies, Vol. 2* (4th edition). London: Routledge & Kegan Paul.

Proust, M. (1913–27). *Remembrance of things past* (C. K. Scott-Moncreiff, T. Kilmartin, & A. Mayor, Trans.). London: Chatto & Windus (current edition 1981).

Quinton, D., & Rutter, M. (1988). *Parenting breakdown: The making and breaking of inter-generational links*. Aldershot: Avebury.

Quinton, D., Rutter, M., & Liddle, C. (1984). Institutional rearing, parental difficulties and marital support. *Psychological Medicine, 14,* 107–124.

Raleigh, M. J., McGuire, M. T., Brammer, G. L., Pollack, D. B., & Yuwiler, A. (1991). Serotonergic mechanisms promote dominance acquisition in adult male vervet monkeys. *Brain Research, 559,* 181–190.

Reddy, W. M. (2001). *The navigation of feeling: A framework for the history of emotions*. New York: Cambridge University Press.

Rimé, B. (1998). Address of the Retiring President, International Society for Research on Emotions. Würzburg.

Rimé, B., Finkenauer, C., Luminet, O. Zech, E., & Philippot, P. (1998). Social sharing of emotion: New evidence and new questions. *European Review of Social Psychology, 9,* 145–189.

Rogers, C.R. (1972). My personal growth. In A. Burton & Associates (Eds.) *Twelve therapists* (pp. 28–77). San Francisco: Jossey-Bass.

Rogers, H.E. (1965). A wife's-eye view of Carl Rogers. *Voices, 1,* 93–98.

Rosenberg, R., & Bloom, H. (1990). *The book of J*. New York: Grove Weidenfeld.

Rosenwein, B. H. (2002). Worrying about emotions in history. *American Historical Review, 107,* 821–845.

Rousseau, J.-J. (1750). Discourse on the question: Has the restoration of the arts and sciences been conducive to the purification of morals? *The essential Rousseau* (L. Bair, Ed., pp. 203–230). New York: Penguin-New American Library (current edition 1975).

Rozin, P., Haidt, J., & McCauley, C. R. (2000). Disgust. In M. Lewis & J. M. Haviland-Jones (Eds.), *Handbook of emotions* (2nd edition, pp. 637–653). New York: Guilford.

Russell, J. A. (2003). Core affect and the psychological construction of emotion. *Psychological Review, 110,* 145–172.

Rutter, M. (1972). *Maternal deprivation reassessed.* Harmondsworth: Penguin.

Salovey, P. (2003). Emotional intelligence: What do we really know? Paper presented at the American Psychological Association Annual Convention, Toronto.

Salovey, P., & Mayer, J. (1990). Emotional intelligence. *Imagination, Cognition and Personality, 9,* 185–211.

Salovey, P., Kokkonen, M., Lopes, P. N., & Mayer, J. D. (2004). Emotional intelligence: What do we know? In A. S. R. Manstead, N. H. Frijda, & A. H. Fischer (Eds.), *Feelings and emotions: The Amsterdam Symposium* (pp. 321–340). Cambridge: Cambridge University Press.

Schank, R., & Abelson, R. (1977). *Scripts, plans, goals and understanding: An inquiry into human knowledge structures.* Hillsdale, NJ: Erlbaum.

Scheff, T. J. (1997). *Emotions, the social bond, and human reality: Part/whole analysis.* New York: Cambridge University Press.

Seligman, M. E. P. (2002). *Authentic happiness: Using the new positive psychology to realize your potential for lasting fulfilment.* New York: Free Press.

Shallice, T., & Burgess, P. W. (1991). Deficits in strategy application following frontal lobe damage in man. *Brain, 114,* 727–741.

Sherif, M., & Sherif, C. W. (1953). *Groups in harmony and in tension.* New York: Harper & Row.

Shermer, M. (2003). The domesticated savage. *Scientific American, 289*(3), 40.

Shields, S. A. (2002). *Speaking from the heart: Gender and the social meaning of emotion.* Cambridge: Cambridge University Press.

Shorter, E. (1997). *A history of psychiatry.* Toronto: Wiley.

Shostrom, E. L. (Producer) (1966). Three approaches to psychotherapy (film). Santa Ana, CA: Psychological Films.

Smith, A. (1759). *The theory of moral sentiments.* Oxford: Oxford University Press (current edition 1976).

Snow, J. (1855). *On the mode of communication of cholera* (2nd edition, much enlarged). London: Churchill.

Sorabji, R. (2000). *Emotion and peace of mind: From Stoic agitation to Christian temptation*. Oxford: Oxford University Press.

Spinoza, B. (1661–75). *On the improvement of the understanding, The ethics, and Correspondence* (R. H. M. Elwes, Trans.). New York: Dover (modern edition 1955).

Stanovich, K. (2004). *The robot's rebellion: Finding meaning in the age of Darwin*. Chicago: University of Chicago Press.

Stearns, P. N. (1999). *Battleground of desire: The struggle for self-control in modern America*. New York: New York University Press.

Stearns, P. N., & Stearns, C. Z. (1985). Emotionology: Clarifying the history of emotions and emotional standards. *American Historical Review, 90*, 813–886.

Sternberg, R. H. (2004). *The nature of pity*. New York: Cambridge University Press.

Stockdale, J. B. (1995a). Testing Epictetus's doctrines in a laboratory of human behavior. *Bulletin of the Institute of Classical Studies, 40*, 1–13.

Stockdale, J. B. (1995b). *Thoughts of a philosophical fighter pilot*. Stanford, CA: Hoover Institution Press.

Stone, L. (1977). *The family, sex and marriage in England 1500–1800*. London: Weidenfeld & Nicolson.

Taine, H. (1882) *De l'intelligence, Tome 2*. Paris: Hachette.

Tangney, J. P., & Dearing, R. L. (2002). *Shame and guilt*. New York: Guilford.

Tetlock, D. (Trans.). (1985). *Popol Vuh*. New York: Simon & Schuster.

Tomkins, S. S. (1970). Affect as the primary motivational system. In M. B. Arnold (Ed.), *Feelings and emotions: The Loyola Symposium* (pp. 101–110). New York: Academic Press.

Tomkins, S. S. (1979). Script theory: Differential magnification of affects. In H. E. Howe & R. A. Dienstbier (Eds.), *Nebraska Symposium on Motivation, 1978* (Vol. 26, pp. 201–236). Lincoln, NB: University of Nebraska Press.

Tomkins, S. S. (1995). *Exploring affect: The selected writings of Sylvan S. Tomkins* (E.V. Demos, Ed.). New York: Cambridge University Press.

Tooby, J., & Cosmides, L. (1990). The past explains the present: Emotional adaptations and the structure of ancestral environments. *Ethology and Sociobiology, 11*, 375–424.

Waters, E., Merrick, S., Treboux, D., Crowell, J., & Albersheim, L. (2000). Attachment security in infancy and early adulthood: A twenty-year longitudinal study. *Child Development, 71*, 684–689.

Watson, J. D., & Crick, F. H. C. (1953). Molecular structure of nucleic acids: A structure for deoxyribose nucleic acid. *Nature, 171*, 727–728.

Webster, C. (1995). Computer modeling of adaptive depression. *Behavioral Science, 40*, 314–330.

Weinfield, N. S., Sroufe, A., & Egeland, B. (2000). Attachment from infancy to early adulthood in a high risk sample: Continuity, discontinuity, and their correlates. *Child Development, 71*, 695–702.

Winnicott, D. W. (1971). *Playing and reality*. Harmondsworth: Penguin.

Wordsworth, W. (1802). Preface to *Lyrical Ballads* of 1802. In S. Gill (Ed.) (1984), *William Wordsworth* (pp. 595–615). Oxford: Oxford University Press.

Wrangham, R. (2001). Out of the *Pan,* into the fire: How our ancestors' evolution depended on what they ate. In F. de Waal (Ed.), *Tree of origin: What primate behavior can tell us about human social evolution* (pp. 121–143). Cambridge, MA: Harvard University Press.

Wright, R. (1992). *Stolen continents: The "New World" through Indian eyes*. Toronto: Penguin Canada.

Zeldin, T. (1994). *An intimate history of humanity*. London: Sinclair Stevenson.

Zeldin, T. (1998). *Conversation*. London: Harvill Press.

Name Index

Subject Index

188 SUBJECT INDEX

8732

DISCARD